Is **Dating**

your road map to

Engagement?

Is **Dating**

your road map to

Engagement?

Biblical insights on relationships,
premarital sex, purity, engagement,
and how we can live for the Lord

Foreword by
His Grace Bishop Moussa

George M. Bassaly, M.D.

St. John Book Center
2007

All scripture quotations, unless otherwise indicated, are taken from the New King James Version®. Copyright © 1982 by Thomas Nelson, Inc. Used by permission. All rights reserved.

Scripture taken from the NEW AMERICAN STANDARD BIBLE®, Copyright © 1960, 1962, 1963, 1968, 1971, 1972, 1973, 1975, 1977, 1995 by The Lockman Foundation. Used by permission.

Copyright © 2007 by George M. Bassaly

All rights reserved. No part of this book may be reproduced or transmitted in any form or by any means, electronic or mechanical, including photocopying, recording or by an information storage and retrieval system, without prior written permission from the writer.

ISBN: 0-9795664-0-1
ISBN-13: 978-0-9795664-0-0

Distributed by:
   St. John Book Center
   stjohnbookcenter@gmail.com

Dedication

To His Holiness Pope Shenouda III

Who loves the Lord God with all his heart, with all his soul, and with all his mind.
Who tirelessly serves his flock until Christ is formed in them.
Who believes that a Church without youth is a Church without a future.

Our Lord and Savior Jesus Christ

St. Mark the Evangelist

His Holiness
Pope Shenouda III

The One Hundred and Seventeenth Pope of Alexandria and Patriarch of the See of St. Mark the Evangelist

Contents

Forewords viii

Acknowledgments x

Introduction xi

1. The Man-Woman Relationship 1
2. Pressure from Society 7
3. Is Your Friendship Crossing the Line? 17
4. Be Holy in All Your Conduct 23
5. Dating and Its Effects 39
6. Dating a Non-Christian 49
7. Cohabitation 59
8. Premarital Sex 67
9. Studies and Statistics on Sexual Behaviors 81
10. Called to Be Different 89
11. How to Be Different 99
12. Living in Purity 109
13. Steps to Engagement 117
14. A Time for Every Purpose 129
15. Advice in Deciding Whom to Marry 137
16. Pitfalls in Choosing Whom to Marry 149
    Concluding Thoughts 156

Forewords

Coptic Orthodox Patriarchate
Youth Bishopric

This book is the result of many studies and experiences of Dr. George Bassaly. He has been working with the youth and young adults for many years, and in churches of many countries.

This is why this book came into print, responding to the needs of our young people, and answering all the important questions that they raised at their meetings, such as:

- Why is there an attraction to the opposite sex?
- Is dating accepted Biblically and socially?
- What about premarital sex?
- How do I choose my life partner?
- When should I start the marriage process?

Thanks to Dr. George Bassaly for his efforts. I wish the best for our beloved youth, through the prayers of His Holiness Pope Shenouda III.

> Bishop Moussa
> Youth Bishopric
> Coptic Orthodox Church

Coptic Orthodox Church of St. George
Sporting, Alexandria, Egypt

In this book, Dr. Bassaly shares his many years of experience, fellowship and love with the youth and young adults, with a Biblical and practical approach. He lifts up the heart of the reader to heaven, without overlooking the different emotional, social, physical and spiritual aspects of his or her life.

He believes in a well-balanced life without dualism. He writes with his heart and mind, with a Biblical perspective, a candid honesty, in a captivating and pleasant style.

This book is essential for anyone who wishes to experience an inner joy, with sound personality founded in Jesus Christ, the true friend of every person.

Rev. Fr. Tadros Y. Malaty
March 16, 2007
New Jersey, USA

Acknowledgments

First and foremost, I would like to thank our Lord and Savior Jesus Christ who allowed this book to be written. Without His grace and His work in us, this project would not have come to fruition.

I am honored that His Grace Bishop Moussa reviewed the book, and kindly agreed to write a foreword. With deep gratitude, I thank him for his encouragement and inspiration. His service, among the youth and adults, is very much esteemed and appreciated.

My sincere thanks are addressed to Rev. Fr. Tadros Y. Malaty, who originally had presented the idea of this project. It is also a privilege that he reviewed the book, wrote a foreword, and offered his unwavering support.

I am indebted to John Gabriel, M.D., for his proofreading, editing and commenting. His long hours and exhaustive reviews helped refine the book to its best possible form.

Also, special thanks go to all the youth, young adults, and adults across the continents, for all their advice, suggestions, and help. It is almost impossible to enumerate each and every name, but the many hours I spent with them were invaluable.

Finally, a heart filled appreciation to all my relatives and friends who prayed for this venture. They were a source of encouragement when this project seemed to be endless.

May our Lord and Savior Jesus Christ reward all those who contributed, in the heavenly kingdom.

Introduction

Dating, for many, is perceived as a necessity. They argue that without dating, they will not be able to find the right spouse. However, dating comes with many illusions and temptations that cause people to stumble, and stray from their initial intention. On the other hand, if the process of getting to know someone is approached circumspectly, the outcome can be quite rewarding. But, how is one to find their way through such a difficult and illusive maze.

This book attempts to shed light on dating, as well as the subjects of the man-woman relationship, friendships, premarital sex, purity, and more. Furthermore, it provides what the writer hopes you will find to be valuable guidance for couples taking the steps leading to engagement – with honesty, purity, and sincerity.

The following is a list of some of the many issues and topics discussed.

- Why do we get attracted to the opposite sex?
- What are the pressures of society and their effects?
- Is having a good time with the opposite sex wrong?
- Is dating Biblically and spiritually sound?
- What is wrong in having premarital sex?
- Are Christians supposed to be different than anyone else?
- Is it wrong to date a non-Christian?
- How can I remain chaste and pure for the Lord?
- When is the right time to think of marriage?
- How can I choose my future husband/wife?
- What are the pitfalls in choosing a husband/wife?

As you read, let the Holy Spirit guide your heart, mind, and soul to hear His voice, and live according to His word. I do hope that you will find answers to many of your questions. May the Lord guide you to all wisdom and spiritual understanding.

N.B. Please note that names in the stories were changed for confidentiality.

Italics are used for emphasis.

1

The Man-Woman Relationship

In order to understand the essence of the man-woman relationship, we need to refer back to the story of creation. Early in the Bible, we read about Adam, and how he was enjoying the presence of God, as He fulfilled all his needs. Then, in Genesis 2:18 we read, "And the LORD God said, "*It is* not good that man should be alone; I will make him a helper comparable to him." God manifested His love to Adam by creating another human being, a helper, comparable to him with whom he could relate, and share life. Moreover, God did not intend them to be a mere "couple," but to actually be bound as one. This special bond is also a means for us to understand God's true and unconditional love toward us, His creation. The Bible did not say that the two shall become very intimate, but *one flesh* (Genesis 2:24; Matthew 19:6). This oneness is a mystery, blessed and sanctified by the Holy Spirit.

Out of His love, God blessed their union, and the entire human race. He wanted them to enjoy a truly joyful, peaceful, and blessed union. God is perfect and, through His love, He provided perfect plans for the human race. Everything God created was good in every sense.

Affinity

Part of God's perfect plan was creating us with an affinity toward the opposite sex. This attraction is not a sinful one; it is a normal physiological phenomenon. However, what matters is how one construes this attraction, which will dictate the quality of our relationships. If we base this attraction on worldly standards (forgetting God's intentions for us), we will certainly fall into many temptations, and the relationship will be full of shame, guilt and disappointment. On the other hand, if one bases this attraction on holy standards, then the relationship will be pure and fruitful; leading to a rewarding and enriching life.

Some people misinterpret this attraction as a human need in and of itself. As a result, some may argue that this physical attraction must be satisfied. Through this way of thinking, they live and interact with the opposite sex on the basis of fulfilling those "needs." Again, the attraction that we feel toward the opposite sex is a God given characteristic, and not a need.

Human Needs

There are various behavioral science theories concerning human needs. Nearly, all of these theories agree on certain basic needs that require being satisfied, in order for one to live a healthy life. They sustain our physical existence, develop our social aptitude, and enhance our spirituality.

Essential physiological needs are the ones such as food and water. Essential social needs are safety, security, belonging, acceptance and love. We look for acceptance and approval from others, as well as recognition in our community. We generally want to belong to groups where we can share our interests and ambitions. We like to feel needed, wanted and loved. Apart from this need to be a part of some social group, we also seek someone with whom we can share our life. It is important to understand that we need to be at a certain level of maturity (physical, psychological, intellectual, and spiritual) to be able to discern and choose the right person with whom we will share life.

Here, it is vital to draw our attention to our spiritual needs. Their importance can't be overemphasized. *They take precedence over all other needs.* In fact, addressing our spiritual needs will put everything else into proper perspective.

At this stage, it is worth mentioning that there are some people who choose to live a celibate life. They strive to fulfill a higher calling of spirituality – whether they are in the world or in monasteries or in convents. Their main concern is the love of the Lord and how to fully live for Him. That level of spirituality may transcend many of the above mentioned needs.

Subject or Object

What attracts us to the opposite sex is generally their appearance, demeanor, beliefs or status. As was mentioned, this attraction is a normal physiological phenomenon, and God instilled it in us to fulfill His divine plan.

God did not create Adam and Eve to simply have them fulfill their biological and physical needs. He had other plans for them. However, humanity, in pursuing its own selfish desires, allowed sin to corrupt its nature. These tarnished desires lead some people to get carried away to the point of perceiving each other as objects – to fulfill their own biological and physical desires. Genesis 6:12 reads, "So God looked upon the earth, and indeed it was corrupt; for all flesh had corrupted their way on the earth."

Regretfully, we have degraded a wonderfully created human figure to an object of man's pleasure. Movies, television, music and magazines incessantly reinforce the idea that men and women are not to be respected, but to be used. Note that this portrayal is not always overtly presented by the media, but often subtly implied. Sadly, with all these influences, men and women's perceptions of each other are distorted from those of subjects, to mere objects – to be used and exploited.

Now, did God leave men and women to their own minds and feelings? No, He did not. He sent His only begotten Son, who is the way, the truth, and the life (John 14:6) – to renew, in Him, the human nature that was corrupted by sin.

At this point, it is worthwhile to mention about the Virgin Mary. She was chaste and pure. Will men be able to look at women and imagine that the Virgin Mary could have been one of them? Will it be possible for men and women to think that they could be pure and chaste as she? With this pure eye, men and women can see each other the way God intended them to be. Neither men nor women are of lower creatures that they should look at each other with lustful and wanton passion. Let us respect each other, and look at the human race through God's pure and loving eyes.

How Do We Interact with Each Other?

We need to ask ourselves a couple of questions: "How do we see and interact with the opposite sex? Do we treat them as God-given gifts and helpers?" The way men and women view each other will surely influence how they interact and communicate. As was mentioned, society has a lot to do with the demoralized view of how men and women perceive each other. We end up disrespecting, mistreating, and hurting one another. However, this was not the original intention of our heavenly Father. The Holy Spirit teaches us through St. Paul, saying, "*Be* kindly affectionate to one another with brotherly love, in honor giving preference to one another" (Romans 12:10).

The following are some characteristics and standards by which we ought to view and treat each other:

- as brothers and sisters in Christ
- with a pure mind
- not as mere bodies and objects
- as helpers
- with sound morals
- with genuineness, respect and trustworthiness
- having a sound personality
- as caring and loving Christians
- with a spirit of forgiveness

If we remember these godly viewpoints, our interactions and relationships with the opposite sex will certainly be pure and honest. On the contrary, if we let our perspective get swayed by the world, then the way we treat each other will not be in accordance to our God. Our Lord and Savior Jesus Christ overcame the world, and we need to let Him, the Good Shepherd, lead our lives. He will help us overcome the world, and all its temptations.

"These things I have spoken to you, that in Me you may have peace. In the world you will have tribulation; but be of good cheer, I have overcome the world" (John 16:33).

In the next chapter, we will discuss how society and the media may shape our thoughts and attitudes.

♦ ♦ ♦ ♦ ♦ ♦ ♦

"So Jacob served seven years for Rachel, and they seemed *only* a few days to him because of the love he had for her" (Genesis 29:20).

2

Pressure from Society

Society has a lot to do with the way we act and interact with our surroundings. Our clothing, cars, hairstyles, and even the way we talk, usually reflect what is perceived to be preferable to society at that point in time. However, what is preferable to society is not always right.

St. Paul said, "All things are lawful for me, but all things are not helpful. All things are lawful for me, but I will not be brought under the power of any" (1 Corinthians 6:12). "All things are lawful for me, but not all things are helpful; all things are lawful for me, but not all things edify" (1 Corinthians 10:23). He describes the fact that all things may be acceptable, but not everything will edify him, nor will he be under the control of any. Society, with all its pressures, could not lord over his life, and control the way he wanted to live for the Savior.

We may not be as conscientious as St. Paul, and at times, we behave as followers and emulate others without giving our actions much thought. In other words, we may make others' practices our own, for no good reason other than to join the crowd, or to avoid being different. Those who don't conform to the majority's standards are often looked at differently. The result is that we are often faced with the dilemma, and sometimes a struggle, of choosing between conforming to societal norms, and holding on to what is right. To help keep ourselves on the right track, we constantly need to be aware of:

- What is leading us?
- Why are we followers?
- Is what we are doing Biblically correct?

Those who opt to do what's "easy" are those who may not have a stronger personality, and may not stand the notion that they would be different. As a result, their views and values tend to be wavering. On the other hand, those who choose to do what's right, tend to have stronger convictions, which will keep their ideals from swaying.

Early Influences

As we steer through life, we go through so many different experiences; and many of our behaviors are molded as a result of those experiences. The way we handle the different challenges we will face are, to a great extent, based on those early experiences and lessons. Furthermore, how we interpret our experiences is significantly affected by our upbringing. It is this early learning that will have a determining factor on how we think of ourselves, how we perceive the world, and how we react to our environment. Therefore, a God-fearing upbringing during that early period of life is of prime importance.

As an illustration, there was a father who once asked for guidance concerning his sixteen-year-old son, who was drifting away from the right path. The father explained that his son had not been to church since he was six, and that he himself was extremely busy with his business and various pursuits. His son did not have someone to offer him spiritual guidance and support. He was never encouraged to attend Church, participate in the Holy Mysteries, and be involved in the different activities. There is a lot of truth to the old adage, "A family that prays together stays together."

How do you expect this young man's life (or any of our lives) to turn out if he did not have an effective relationship with God, early in his life? He was not offered the opportunity of knowing God, and letting Him work in his life. He did not have the Lord as his cornerstone in the face of society's influences.

That's not to say that there is no hope for people who don't seek God early in their lives. Many people meet the Lord later in life, and continue to enjoy a blessed relationship with Him. However, knowing the Lord early in one's life, and growing in Him, will have a deeper impact on the individual. In addition, the individual would have enjoyed a longer period of a blessed relationship with the Lord. This longer period would have deepened and broadened his scope of spirituality (from prayers, readings, fasting, spiritual exercises, and more). Thus, a more fruitful relationship with God is formed, and a stronger stand is established, as one faces the world.

Self-Image and Rejection

We want to feel that we belong to some place or group, or even to just one individual. We would like to avoid the pain of being left out. Living with rejection is difficult to accept. Many people may compromise their own identity for the sake of being accepted by their friends. Wendy, 23, once described putting on a "facemask" whenever she was with her friends. She was trying to be as pleasant and conforming as possible, in an effort to be accepted by them. There are many reasons for behaving in such a manner. Trying to please others may be due to a lack of fulfillment, love, security or trust in our lives. It is an attempt to try to fill a void in life with the feeling of acceptance.

Influence of the Media

Clever advertisements and commercials suggest the kind of outfits we are to wear, the kind of jokes we are to say, and how we ought to behave. The attitudes of today's media heroes and superstars permeate our minds. From the moment we wake up we are bombarded with words, images, and temptations – whether implicit or explicit. Turn on the radio and you will soon be listening to immoral words and stories. Watch television and you will be exposed to the same recurring issues of violence, premarital sex, adultery, sexual expressiveness, infidelity, etc. Without being completely aware of its influences, the media affects our views on life, sexuality, and relationships. The media also may provide us with a false sense of self-assurance, pleasure, confidence, power, health, and even a sense of who we are. We are also deceived into believing that these "desirables" can provide us with everything we need and want, leading to our happiness. It not only suggests how we should live, but also fills us with a sense of pride and self-centeredness – "It is only me that counts."

Our society is becoming so materialistic, sex-oriented, and self-oriented, to the point that it is very difficult for men and women to stay pure and virgin.

If you have been lulled into accepting this worldly view, do not be discouraged. Contrary to these waves of moral decline, there are rays of light among us – people who want to live a holy and sanctified life in the presence of God and His angels. We can find encouragement and inspiration in their way of life.

We were not created with a sinful nature. Yet, we were created with free will. On the other hand, when Adam was confronted with temptation, he chose disobedience and sin. Nevertheless, God did not leave this human nature desolate, nor did He leave it in the hands of the world, or Satan. He sent His Holy Spirit to comfort, strengthen and guide us. "However, when He, the Spirit of truth, has come, He will guide you into all truth…" (John 16:13).

Let's discuss a few specific examples of ways the media influences us.

Television

Let's say that, on average, we watch one hour of television per day, and therefore at least 10 commercials. That translates to approximately 3600 advertisements per year! That much exposure, and repetition, will surely have their effects on an individual. People often eat, sleep, study, converse, and even read the Bible while the television is turned on! We become slaves to this loud machine. What does the television really show us? Mostly what we watch, are food and product advertisements, violence, obscene language, sexually explicit behavior, news, sports, and sometimes, educational materials. Note that besides the news, sports, and the educational materials, the other subject matters are mainly geared toward our instincts and sensual matters. Studies have shown that nearly 70% of what is aired by national broadcast television stations has some sexual content.

Television also gives us the false impression that the real life is what is portrayed in some of its programs. The way in which its actors respond to life events may *seem* appropriate. Therefore we are lulled into believing that this is the way we should conduct our lives. Unfortunately, we are sometimes dazzled by their glamorous lives, and wish to attain their unrealistic and often unhealthy life style.

The television itself is not evil, but one should discern which broadcasts are harmful from those that are edifying. You may watch a program for only ten minutes, and your soul and spirit may be edified.

On the other hand, the effects of ten minutes of a damaging program may stay with you for a very long time. Certain images and scenes may stay in our memory and subconscious for many years! We may think that these scenes do not affect us while watching them, but sooner or later, they certainly will affect us in some way.

Sorrowfully, watching television has become an addiction to many. The point again is discernment: choosing properly to what we subject ourselves, and having limits to the time we spend in front of the television. Finally, we need to live according to the commandments of God, and His statutes, to lead a truly successful and joyful life.

Music

Music is constantly in our environment – at home, in the car, at work, in shopping malls, and in restaurants. When we listen to certain songs frequently, we may start repeating the words out of memory; the words may then take root in our souls. Slowly, the song's message becomes an attitude, then a lifestyle.

There are many varieties of music. Some types are beneficial, while others can have a profoundly detrimental effect on us. Knowing that many songs we hear today address sex and sensual relationships, we can imagine how their lyrics may affect us. It was once said of a composer and songwriter that the music of the mid–20th century addressed the soul, but that of the late–20th century was geared toward the body.

Imagine meeting your potential future spouse after listening to sensually oriented music for hours. All the messages you elicited from those songs are now stored in your mind, and will tend to be expressed in some way. What you had subjected yourself to, will influence the way you look, talk, think and behave with that person. The lyrics and the music will likely preoccupy your mind, and will have a great influence on your behavior and your expectations.

Compare that situation with a couple that meets with a pure mind, after they had prayed for God's guidance – before they got together. Will their minds go astray to think of ungodly and immoral thoughts? It is still possible; but compared to the former situation, it is far less likely. They will be more equipped to resist temptation through the Holy Spirit working in them.

A good example on the effect of this harmful music could be taken from the writings of one of the early Church Fathers, St. John Chrysostom (4th century A.D.). He asked his congregation to remove from their lives disgraceful and "satanic" music. He even went a step further, by asking his people not to associate themselves with those who take pleasure in such dissolute entertainment. He emphasized, back in the fourth century, the same message of discerning between good and evil, pure and impure, holy and defiled.

We need to listen to Him instead of the music that stirs up our lusts.

"This people I have formed for Myself; They shall declare My praise" (Isaiah 43:21).

"speaking to one another in psalms and hymns and spiritual songs, singing and making melody in your heart to the Lord" (Ephesians 5:19).

Internet

You can search innumerable topics and get a vast array of information from the World Wide Web. You can search whole libraries, plan vacations, communicate with others, and even shop online. It can be a great tool if it is used properly.

On the other hand, you might find yourself engaged in inappropriate discussions in a chat room, or you may find a date online. You may come across an adult website, or get scammed by misleading advertisements. We also know how people can get so attached to certain websites, like Facebook and MySpace.

Furthermore, whether one is subject to the damaging aspects of the Internet, or searching for general information, one may simply stay online for many hours. This habit may easily become an addiction that is difficult to remedy.

If the Internet is not used properly, it may demoralize a person, and alter the way he thinks and behaves. We need to evaluate what we are going to reap from all the time spent in front of the computer screen.

Whom to Follow

The suggestion here is not that everyone turns off their radios, televisions, and computers. It is by using discernment and firmness; we can train ourselves how to live the heavenly life on earth.

In Philippians 3:8, St. Paul takes us to higher and higher levels of spirituality and holiness. He tells us, "Yet indeed I also count all things loss for the excellence of the knowledge of Christ Jesus my Lord, for whom I have suffered the loss of all things, and count them as rubbish, that I may gain Christ." The more one tastes the sweetness of the Lord, and grows in His knowledge, the more one feels that everything else is a waste.

In the Old Testament, we read about the prophet Elijah in 1 Kings 18:21, "And Elijah came to all the people, and said, 'How long will you falter between two opinions? If the LORD *is* God, follow Him; but if Baal, follow him.' But the people answered him not a word." In other words, I should not be wavering between living for God for sometime, and then living for the world in other times. I should follow Him wholeheartedly.

The Lord does not want us to be with Him for one hour, and resort to the world's ways the next. We are all sinners and are weak; but such wavering does not show our dedication and commitment to Him. We may make mistakes daily, but we need to return to Him in repentance, and ask for forgiveness.

Conclusion

As you can see, there are many strong influences that affect our intentions, views, and conduct. Our society, friends, and certainly the media, affect us in ways that may not be edifying.

One of the things that may certainly get deleteriously affected is the man-woman relationship. We need to be careful and take note of what is influencing our ideals. It is of special significance when it comes to our perception and purpose of our relationships with the opposite sex.

We want to live our lives in light of the Bible and find out what the word of God is telling us: to live a holy and sanctified life for Him. The pressure will surely be constant, but the Lord Himself, the Creator, is with us. He is stronger than any pressure or influence we may face.

Too late did I love Thee, O Fairness,
so ancient, and yet so new!

Too late did I love Thee! For behold,
Thou were within, and I without,

And there did I seek Thee

Thou were with me,
but I was not with Thee.

Thou called, and cried aloud,
and forced open my deafness.

Thou didst gleam and shine,
and chase away my blindness.

Thou didst touch me,
and I burned for Thy peace.

When I shall cleave unto Thee
with all my being,

then shall I in nothing
have pain and labor;

and my life shall be a real life,
being wholly full of Thee.

St. Augustine (Confessions)

3

Is Your Friendship Crossing the Line?

Joy, 23, was involved with a "friend," Ted, 24. Her friends noticed that she is not "all there" when she's with them. Joy responded, "I don't know why you all keep insisting that I am interested in him. Why don't you believe me when I tell you that there is nothing going on with Ted? He's just a friend."

Although Joy might truly believe he is just a friend, she may have slowly developed feelings for him. Most likely she had spent a lot of time with him, started to think of him, and talk about him. Her friends probably noticed a change in her behavior when he's around, or when his name comes up in conversation.

Her friendship had evolved into a different kind of relationship. Either she is in complete denial, or she is ignoring the issue altogether. Had she noticed the signs that her friendship was getting to a more intimate stage, she would not have been on the defensive. She was actually attempting to hide the fact that there was something between the two of them.

Is it Possible to Be Just Friends?

Yes, it is. You can have friends of the opposite sex with honesty, sincerity, respect and dignity. To maintain a friendship (as brothers and sisters in Christ), you need to set limits and boundaries. Have healthy relationships, but do not be too occupied or consumed by them. Things may get quite difficult once they progress past a certain point. Try not to give intimacy a chance to bud, if you just want to maintain a brotherly Christian friendship. However, if your intentions are to pursue a sincere, potentially lifelong marital relationship with this individual, then that is a totally different situation (will be discussed in later chapters).

One way to ensure that your friendships remain pure, and healthy, is to watch out for "red flags." These indicators may alert you that your relationship may be heading toward an unclear path.

Red Flags

There are many red flags that you should be aware of, but we will only mention a few here.

One of the first things you may notice is that your conversations are lasting for increasingly longer periods of time, leading to an inevitably closer relationship. You may increase the number of phone calls, emails or online chats.

A second red flag is that you are having frequent get-togethers, leading to a progression of the relationship.

(Therefore, at this stage you have engaged two of your senses: hearing and sight).

A third red flag is trying to justify the amount of time you are spending with each other.

You may say that you are helping her with studies or

with work, listening to her problems, or you are just talking.

A common theme to these red flags is the amount of time that is spent in that relationship. The result is that you may then become desensitized to the evolution of the relationship, as intimacy is developing. You may even stop questioning whether the time you are spending together is right or wrong.

At this point you may have involved a third sense, the sense of touch, which creates yet another strong bond. (Now you are subjecting three senses: sight, hearing, and touch). Remember, the more senses that are involved, the stronger the memories, the bond and the emotional attachment.

At this juncture, let's look at how one can set limits on a relationship, to maintain a true Christian friendship.

Setting Limits on Your Friendships

1. *Do not compromise your spiritual growth* by spending most of your time with your friend, and less time with the Lord and church services. Focus on the Lord and your spiritual growth.

2. *Set your moral standards high.* Do not compromise. Prove that you are a true Christian by the way you live, talk and behave with others – since these are true reflections of your relationship with the Lord.

3. *Do not isolate yourselves.* The direction of a one-to-one relationship may become unclear if either party is not mature enough. Spending time in a group setting is much healthier. You will be interacting with several people – not just focusing on one person.

There were two friends who used to serve together at a nursing home. They were so involved in the service – planning things for the elderly, buying food for them, spending time with them, and praying for them. Many people at the Church praised them for their eagerness and dedication. They were just wonderful.

But, in time, instead of looking at the service and its needs, they started looking at their own emotional needs. They began meeting regularly to spend time together, and talk about their relationship. Then, they focused on their desires, which turned lustful.

Needless to say, their service suffered. This went on for some time, and ultimately they left the service altogether. Finally, they broke up and went their separate ways. This sequence of events could have been avoided had they focused on the service, kept their relationship honest, and not isolating themselves.

4. *Be honest.* Ask yourself, regarding your relationship, some questions: Would you feel comfortable telling everyone what is going on between the two of you? Would you take pride in your relationship instead of hiding it? Would you feel uneasy, or even ashamed, if people know what you are doing? Do you really know where you are heading, and where you are leading the other person? Where do you stand in light of the word of God and His commandments?

5. *Always remember who you are.* We are daughters and sons of the King. We should be careful in not spoiling His name or the royal garment we wear. By keeping His words in our hearts, we can live our lives as heavenly and royal people. Psalm 119:11 reads, "Your word I have hidden in my heart, That I might not sin against You." Keep His words in your

heart and mind. They will guard you and remind you of your royal sonship. Memorize as many Bible verses as you can – especially from the Psalms. Your mind will be occupied with the Lord and you will be able to quench all the fiery darts of the devil (Ephesians 6).

6. *Do not neglect your family, career and friends.* They each need special attention and time. Ignoring any one area (i.e. for the sake of a relationship) may lead you to feel dissatisfied with your life.

7. *Seek guidance* from your priests, church leaders, your family and friends. Be attentive, and carefully evaluate their advice. Their guidance and support will be particularly valuable when you are feeling vulnerable. Accountability is critical if you are dependent on a relationship.

8. *Occupy yourself* with healthy, fruitful and edifying tasks that will keep you busy and productive. Boredom can be the spark that can trigger your mind to search for comfort in a relationship, and eventually depend on it. Again, a healthy spiritual and social environment is a necessity.

> "But all things that are exposed are made manifest by the light, for whatever makes manifest is light" (Ephesians 5:13).

4

Be Holy in All Your Conduct

In order to truly understand how we should conduct our lives, we need to refer to the words of God for guidance.

> "Only let your conduct be worthy of the gospel of Christ…" (Philippians 1:27).

> "*Let your* conduct *be* without covetousness…" (Hebrews 13:5).

> "but as He who called you *is* holy, you also be holy in all *your* conduct" (1 Peter 1:15).

> "For this is the will of God, your sanctification: that you should abstain from sexual immorality" (1 Thessalonians 4:3).

Essentially, these verses tell us that our lives and actions are to be held to a godly standard. A standard that is quite different from what society dictates. As Christians, we need to set our minds on things above, not on things on earth (Colossians 3:2), and behave as true citizens of heaven (Philippians 3:20).

Misleading Behavior

First Thessalonians 4:6 says, "that no one should take advantage of and defraud his brother in this matter, because the Lord *is* the avenger of all such, as we also forewarned you and testified." Defraud means:

a) To cheat; to deprive of something by deception or fraud (Merriam-Webster's online dictionary, 10th edition).
b) To manipulate; to take advantage of, or to mislead someone.

If a man goes out with a woman for the sake of being seen with her, or to make someone else jealous, or to see if he can get his hands on her body; then he is defrauding her. Also, if a woman knows that there is a gentleman who likes her (while she has no intention of pursuing a relationship), and she takes advantage of this fact for personal gain (e.g. to boost her ego), she is defrauding him. If one were spiritually-oriented, and used sound logic, one would not be carried away by the thrill of being liked, or loved, by the other person.

A man may talk with a woman saying he needs to discuss a personal situation, or work related issue, with her. His true intention was not simply to talk with her, but to spend more time with her. Her aim is to help him out but, with or without her awareness, she is fueling more of his thoughts and daydreams toward her. He is deceiving her. Also, she needs to wisely and prayerfully discern the different situations that she faces each day. If one has attracted the attention of someone that is not of interest to them, he should then be honest and sincere. He should minimize contact – or no contact at all – in order to avoid further false interpretations of his behavior. Some interactions and relationships seem very innocent, but the truth is that sometimes there exist ulterior motives. Even if our motives are in fact pure and honest, can we always be assured that others' motives are also pure? It needs a discerning mind and spirit to recognize and avoid these situations. The reasons for such situations usually revolve around self-satisfaction. David the prophet spoke against this practice in Psalm 101:7, "He who works deceit shall not dwell within my house; He who tells lies shall not continue in my presence." Remember that we all will be held responsible in front of God if we cause others to stumble. "But whoever causes one of these little ones who believe in Me to stumble, it would be better for him if a millstone were hung around his neck, and he were thrown into the sea" (Mark 9:42).

Our societies and cultures need an awakening. We need to be careful and truthfully examine our motives, and the motives of the person with whom we are interacting. If you do not know whether what you are doing is right or wrong, seek guidance; and the Lord will enlighten your mind to be according to His will. Your life is the image and icon of the Lord Jesus Christ, do not spoil it, or let anyone else spoil it. Instead of harming others, let's try to be a light to them, as our Father in heaven is the Light, and interact as brothers and sisters in Christ.

This is how we should be looking at each other, not as potential conquests, but as human beings for whom the Lord Jesus died and shed His blood on the cross. Remember that you are the son/daughter of the KING OF KINGS AND LORD OF LORDS (Revelation 19:16).

Discern and do not deceive. In every condition and situation ask yourself whether the Lord Jesus will be present with you; and will He find your words and behavior acceptable? How does your behavior compare with what we are instructed in the Bible? If you realize that your demeanor is not appropriate, do not hesitate in returning to the way of the Lord.

"Now we have received, not the spirit of the world, but the Spirit who is from God, that we might know the things that have been freely given to us by God" (1 Corinthians 2:12).

Inordinate Affection

Jennie, 23, mistakenly called her colleague by her friend's name, Jonathan, 29. He was all she ever thought about. The rest of the world hardly existed for her. They had been together for only few months, yet she was totally absorbed by him. They spent a lot of time together in that short time, and she even used to spend weekends at his house. While at work, they used to call each other many times a day, even for only few seconds. They were not engaged, nor were they planning to marry. It was just a romance, an overindulgence of feelings, which became a lustful passion – like we see in Hollywood romance stories.

Six months of that romantic, inflamed relationship had passed, and it was quickly over. Jonathan went to a different state and sent her a farewell card without any explanation!

Can you imagine her heartache, and all she had to go through to recover? She thought that hearing nice words, experiencing elated feelings, always having someone to talk to, and having physical relations with Jonathan, meant, "I love you. You are the only one for me." They had focused on the lustful pleasure of the moment rather than a lifelong commitment, pleasing the Lord.

In Colossians 3:5-6 (King James Version) we read, "Mortify therefore your members which are upon the earth; fornication, uncleanness, inordinate affection, evil concupiscence, and covetousness, which is idolatry: For which things' sake the wrath of God cometh on the children of disobedience." Mortify means "to put to death" (Merriam-Webster's online dictionary, 10th edition). Inordinate (same dictionary) means: "unregulated, exceeding reasonable limits, immoderate." Any kind of affection with such a description is provoking the anger of the Lord. Therefore, it is not just the physical relations that we need to keep in check, but also our inclinations, feelings, emotions and affections. If they are not subjected to the will of God, they will certainly go astray.

> "O LORD, do not rebuke me in Your anger, Nor chasten me in Your hot displeasure"
> (Psalm 6:1).

Jennie's Ruined Plans

When Jennie was asked about her life plans, she argued that as long as she and her friend were in "love," nothing else mattered. She hadn't finished college, as she repeatedly postponed her graduation date. She did not plan for a career. All her energy was focused toward that "love" that she had for him. She spent hours thinking and dreaming of him, talking about him, and pleasing and appeasing him (their relationship was often on the edge). They were so centered on their relationship – meeting each other's emotional and physical desires – that they could not appreciate anyone or anything else in their lives. Their relationship became a closed circle in which two bodies were satisfying sinful passions.

Jennie thought she could own Jonathan for good. However, after six months of that infatuation, he abandoned her and she was left feeling hurt, guilty, lonely, worthless and even suicidal. She blamed herself for not being able to make him happy enough! She ended up dropping out of evening classes to deal with her sadness. During their absorbing relationship, Jennie had not been able to heed anyone's advice. She had not been able to accept the fact that she was handling her life carelessly. She had tried to find fulfillment in her relationship with Jonathan, but she was left with emptiness. All her hopes and dreams had vanished.

Head or Heart

Many of our thoughts on morality and sexual involvement are derived from our teenage years, which were filled with emotions and immature inclinations. These emotions and inclinations may result in behaviors that may stay with us for many years. However, would you prefer to be led by your mind, or your heart? In other words, would you rather make decisions based on your emotions, or your thoughts and reasoning? Hopefully you answered "reasoning," which needs to be guided by the Holy Spirit. Decisions based on spiritually inspired thoughts are far more enduring than those based on mere emotions. If you let your feelings and emotions, which could be fleeting, guide your life, you will likely be in for a bumpy, problem-filled journey.

A man and woman may meet, and feel so happy because they share many things in common. From their first encounter, they are convinced that there is "chemistry" between them. Does this mean that they should get married? Will she be the right person for him, and vice versa? This definitely may not be the case.

Someone else, in the same situation, may scrutinize whether this person they have met is right for them. He will also give time for the relationship to ripen, pray about it, and try to get to know the other person better, in different circumstances. Will his emotions be completely shut off? Surely not, he does want to be with her, and spend as much time with her as possible. However, he is using his mind, while leaving room for his emotions and feelings to grow – seeing how the Lord will guide him.

Getting back to Jennie's example, her plans were governed primarily by her heart and desires, which turned lustful. She disregarded her relationship with God and His caring and loving plans for her. She wanted the momentary pleasure – that was all she cared about. She was being led by what satisfied her, not giving a chance for her mind to think properly, nor heeding to its advice. She was unable to see beyond the small world she was living in, and completely nullified any thought of mending her ways, and separating from him. In so doing, she ruined any potentially good plans with which God wanted to bless her.

Trust in God with Patience

We need to trust in God, who takes care of the minute details of our lives. In Jennie's case, she did not wait on God, but hastily went ahead with her own plans. God, out of His great love, has a perfect plan for everyone to be carried out at His perfectly chosen time. Abraham, in the Old Testament, wondered how God promised him that he, and his wife Sarah, would bear children at their advanced age. God's promise was fulfilled a couple of decades later. Does this mean we are to wait decades for God to answer our prayers? Not necessarily, but there is a time under the sun for the Almighty's plan to be revealed to His beloved children (Genesis 17).

We may often rush to what we think will make us feel good, and to where we will feel loved. It is only the Lord who can fill our hearts – with an everlasting love and joy. God has promised to provide the best for us. Wait upon the Lord, and be patient. Do not be pressured by the media, friends, or family. He created you and He will not leave you. "But the very hairs of your head are all numbered. Do not fear therefore; you are of more value than many sparrows" (Matthew 10:30-31). Do not forget that He died for you on the cross. In Romans 5:7-8, it is written, "For scarcely for a righteous man will one die; yet perhaps for a good man someone would even dare to die. But God demonstrates His own love toward us, in that while we were still sinners, Christ died for us." We are His sheep and we need to trust in Him wholeheartedly, knowing the fact that He will guide us to the green pastures – to Himself – where we can find rest.

Morals in Life

Many people do not take into consideration that their inner intentions and desires will ultimately dictate their behavior, and how they relate to others. The following are some Biblical verses and definitions, explaining some unacceptable desires and behaviors, which could be easily overlooked.

> "Now the works of the flesh are manifest, which are these; Adultery, fornication, uncleanness, lasciviousness…that they which do such things shall not inherit the kingdom of God" (Galatians 5:19-21, KJV).

In the NKJV, "lasciviousness" is replaced by "lewdness."

The Merriam-Webster's online dictionary, 10th edition, defines it as wantonness, lust. The Cambridge International Dictionary of English describes it as: expressing a strong desire for sexual activity. Other definitions are: *preoccupied with or exhibiting lustful desires*; playful, unchaste.

A lascivious person is the one who is preoccupied with sex. The same applies if you are consumed with the idea of physical relations with the opposite sex.

We can stir up sexual desires by touching, looking at someone in a suggestive way, or by the type of clothes we wear. We could also stir up these sexual desires by the words we say. For example, our comments or jokes may have double meanings – one of which may have a sexual undertone. These, "apparently" innocent remarks, may very well cause others, as well as ourselves, to stumble. And if we cause anyone to stumble, we are not conducting ourselves in a pure and honest way.

"not in passion of lust, like the Gentiles who do not know God" (1 Thessalonians 4:5).

In the KJV the same verse reads, "Not in lust of concupiscence, even as the Gentiles which know not God."

"Concupiscence" is defined by Merriam-Webster's dictionary as a strong desire (especially sexual). It also means lustful, morbid carnal passion.

Many of our morals are not based on sound spiritual standards or fixed principles, but on shaky ground. If a person's morals are based on worldly principles, then his standards in life will be whatever the world dictates – whether right or wrong. This leads to the question: Who is to say what society dictates is right? Societies differ, customs vary, and behaviors change; while the Bible is right for all people, for all generations, for all times, and for all places. If we do not base our standards on the Bible and Church teachings, we can be certain that our paths will drift from the right track.

"There is a way *that seems* right to a man, But its end *is* the way of death" (Proverbs 14:12; 16:25).

Savor the Time

Another major issue, in this subject of morals and conduct, is how we prioritize our daily commitments and manage our time conscientiously. We keep ourselves busy doing so many insignificant things to the point of exhaustion. We are not able to sit with the Lord, and take in His words.

We feel a sense of responsibility in many areas of our lives, but not so when it comes to our relationship with the Lord. Find time, or rather, make time. Seek the Lord, and He can bless the minutes and hours you spend with Him. Ephesians 5:16 reads, "redeeming the time, because the days are evil."

Savor the time you spend with God. The Bible, your meditations, and your personal time with the Lord are not burdens that you try to get off your back. Do not perceive this time with Him as a duty, but as a privilege, and a grace, to be with your heavenly Father and the heavenly hosts. He is the One to lead your thoughts and actions in the right path. He is your Creator and surely does not want you to live a worldly life, or stray from the right path and lose your peace and joy.

Absolute Truth

Many societies and generations have rejected an absolute standard for what differentiates right from wrong. Many people, whom we know and interact with on a daily basis, claim that absolute truth does not exist – that all truth is relative. Some will say: "What is right for one person, in one situation, might not be right for another." In other words, "Just because it's wrong for you, does not mean it's wrong for me." And since there is no standard, we are easily influenced by popular opinions. The result is a mind-set of accepting what is Biblically wrong. Many people do not challenge this tendency, and become part of the crowd.

Furthermore, we obscure the truth by oversimplifying our actions and deeds, and saying: "It's just a drink." "It's just a joke." "It is just a friendship." "We are just having a good time, so why bother complicating things?"

Among the truths that are obscured are the Christian views on relationships. As a consequence, many eventually think that there is nothing wrong with going out with someone, and engaging in sexual activity.

The number of people accepting inappropriate sexual ideals and behaviors is staggering. You can tell from the news and the despicable stories we hear every day, that our societies and culture are on a downward trend. Compared to twenty or thirty years ago, our generation is more preoccupied, and indulged, with sexual relationships.

In Tune with God

We try to oversimplify things and offer excuses to many of our behaviors, in an effort to avoid the heartache of guilt and sin. This continues to the point of becoming insensitive to the word of God – not hearing or understanding His words. This will then translate as insensitivity to the way we conduct our lives.

Our standards in conducting our lives need to be based on the word of God. A major reason for our society's corruption is the absence of His word in our lives. The further we walk away from living His word, the faster will be our downfall. Being equipped with the word of God will, for sure, safeguard us in making the right decisions in this world and age.

On the other hand, there are people who live far from the Creator, the Lover of mankind, and are doing whatever feels right to them.

> "In those days *there wa*s no king in Israel;
> everyone did *what was* right in his own eyes"
> (Judges 21:25).

We certainly need to be honest with ourselves, and with God. The Lord said,

> "…Inasmuch as these people draw near
> with their mouths And honor Me with their lips,
> But have removed their hearts far from Me, And
> their fear toward Me is taught by
> the commandment of men"
> (Isaiah 29:13).

The world is teaching us erroneous ideals that differ from the Bible, but the Lord wants us to walk in His commandments with love and fear.

> "then I will give them one heart and one way, that they may fear Me forever, for the good of them and their children after them…; but I will put My fear in their hearts so that they will not depart from Me" (Jeremiah 32:39-40).

It is important to note that having sound Biblical beliefs will keep us from falling, but not having Biblical views at all will surely guarantee our fall.

Self-Control

Some people think that since God gave us feelings and hormones, He must be telling us to allow our attractions to control us. That is like saying: "Since God gave me a tongue, I can use it however I can – even to curse. Since God gave me a brain, I can use it to think of evil, and hurt others."

This rationale is certainly erroneous, and also should not apply when talking about our relationships with the opposite sex. We often let our lusts lead our lives, and we end up living destructive lives. We neglect to subdue our lusts so that we live holy for the Lord. "And those *who are* Christ's have crucified the flesh with its passions and desires"

(Galatians 5:24). Self-control is one the fruits of the Holy Spirit (Galatians 5:23).

Unfortunately, we may make decisions to pursue a relationship based on impulsive, superficial and selfish factors. There is little thought given prior to taking those first steps.

> Josephine, 28, was engaged to Keith, 34. He was unsure what to say to her concerning his many past relationships. He was afraid to tell her his stories in the fear that she would lose trust in him, and leave him. He had an impulsive personality, not thinking of future consequences. If he found someone with a different character that attracted him, more than the one whom he was going out with, he would leave her for the sake of the new "lady in town."

He could not commit to any one woman, and his relationship with Josephine started to become unstable. She realized that once he comes across someone else with a different, "more interesting" personality, he would opt to leave her. She finally decided that she could not live with his lack of self-control, and decided to break up with him.

Intimacy without control will lead to sensual stimulations that may not be possible to quench. This relationship will always be hungry for more intimacy. It is like someone filling a glass of wine, and every time it seems empty, he fills it again; and the cycle repeats itself. Living according to the senses may blind the person, and entrap him in Satan's snares.

> Arnold, 40 and married, described how he easily fell into temptation. He said that whenever he used to meet a certain married woman, he was not able to control himself – he always found himself having sex with her. He had wanted a certain lustful momentary pleasure, and he acted

on it. He was sinning against God, himself, his wife, his kids, the other woman, her kids, and her husband! This all happened because he let down his guard. In Ephesians 6:11, it is written, "Put on the whole armor of God, that you may be able to stand against the wiles of the devil." Needless to say Arnold was not able to heed the word of God.

His wife was his lifelong friend and colleague from school. He was asked what will happen if his wife found out about that extramarital affair? He immediately answered that she would commit suicide. She would never have imagined that he would have cheated on her. Was that other woman giving him something more? He used to love his wife, and he says that he still loves her.

He complained that his wife was too preoccupied with the house and kids. Does this fact justify his actions? Surely it does not. He could have been open with his wife, and explained what she was doing to their relationship.

Arnold, as many others would, may say that God let these circumstances happen to him. "If God had really cared, then He would not have let me fall into these temptations."

"Let no one say when he is tempted, 'I am tempted by God'; for God cannot be tempted by evil, nor does He Himself tempt anyone. But each one is tempted when he is drawn away by his own desires and enticed. Then, when desire has conceived, it gives birth to sin; and sin, when it is full-grown, brings forth death" (James 1:13-15).

How can the desire conceive? It is by nurturing it with non-Biblical and immoral ideals. In turn, these ideals will dictate our conduct. In Acts 24:25, we read about St. Paul reasoning with Felix the governor, "Now as he reasoned about righteousness, self-control, and the judgment to come,

Felix was afraid and answered, 'Go away for now; when I have a convenient time I will call for you.' " His fears denoted that his way of life lacked discipline and morals.

Our conduct needs to be well disciplined while trying to live the virtue of self-control. Ask the Lord to bestow upon you this fruit, and in the mean time, be watchful of where your heart and mind are leading you.

May the Lord lead us all to conduct our lives in truth and holiness.

"But we are bound to give thanks to God always for you, brethren beloved by the Lord, because God from the beginning chose you for salvation through sanctification by the Spirit and belief in the truth" (2 Thessalonians 2:13).

5

Dating and Its Effects

The decision to start dating may be the result of societal pressure, or out of a desire to imitate others. In addition, dating, for some, could be a means to satisfy their desires for intimacy and sex. Others date for the sake of having a "good time." Some date because it makes them feel good about themselves – feeling accepted, liked, and loved. Dating may be a means of avoiding loneliness, which can be intolerable for many people. These individuals need to have people around them in order to feel alive. They cannot stand the notion of being alone. Some individuals are so dependent on the existence of someone "special" in their lives, that they can't imagine life without dating. To maintain these feelings, some individuals may jump from one relationship to the next. Then, dating becomes a revolving cycle and an irresistible habit, with consequences that might be overlooked. These people may also be totally preoccupied with thoughts of sex. Sexual relation is to be expected within the first few dates – otherwise it's a sign that things are not going well. For some people, if you do not have sex (or some sort of sexual activity) on the first, third or maybe even the tenth date; the opportunity will always be there, waiting for you. If there is no intimate relation after some time, then you can change partners. If you date and your mind is preoccupied with these thoughts, how long will you be able to resist the powerful emotions and temptations at hand?

Another reason people date stems from the misconception that if they do not date, they would be missing out. They offer rationalizations that they need the "experience" of dating in order to have a successful marriage in the future – irrespective of their age, or level of maturity. They may even consider cohabitation (to be discussed in chapter 7) to "make sure" that they are compatible. The devil certainly plays his role in deceiving people with these illusions.

Once a person starts dating, he may eventually make it a part of his lifestyle. Some may then come to consider dating as an unquestioned and integral part of life – without giving their actions serious and careful thought.

Someone may then ask, "But why should I deprive myself from that intimacy. It feels good to be needed and cared for by someone, and vice versa."

Questions to Consider

The following are questions that may help direct your thoughts regarding dating:

- What will be the main purpose of your relationship? Is it to have "fun"?
- What are your plans for the future regarding that relationship, and what are its potential outcomes?
- What will lead you in your decision making process – your heart, or your "spiritually-oriented mind"?
- Will the words of God in the Bible be your guide?
- Will you be guided by church leaders who truly care about you?

- Will your spiritual growth, and your relationship with the Lord, still be a priority in your life?
- How will you perceive your conduct, and the conduct of your friend, in this relationship; and is it acceptable to the Lord Jesus Christ?

Don't let your desire for intimacy lead you to the hasty decision of getting romantically involved. Carefully consider what's at stake. Don't be led by your emotions and feelings, rather take your time and analyze your situation, using the questions above as a guide.

However, some may argue that they are mature enough to know where they are heading, and are able to differentiate between what is right, from what is wrong. They even attest that their emotions and feelings toward the other individual can be easily controlled. They also add that there is nothing wrong in living like anyone else in society. How long will they be able to resist the devil's traps? Will they succumb to his temptations and deceptions?

You need to seriously, and truthfully, think of the reasons and consequences for going out on a date. The consequences are more problematic than you may think. Try to discover what the will of the Lord is for your life. God will not leave you or forsake you, as you seek Him and His will.

Just Acquaintances

Often, romantic relationships develop out of an innocent acquaintance. This initially superficial relationship may grow over time leading to an outing, and eventually to dating that person. Remember, it is in your hand to let that acquaintance grow, or not. If you let the acquaintance progress, you will need to be mindful of your future plans for that relationship.

If one's initial intentions were innocent, there is still a great chance that the situation may develop into a complex relationship. Both individuals may become emotionally and physically involved. The couple will likely reach a point where neither one knows where, or when, to draw the line. What was "fun" for some time may turn out to be a harmful period in one's life. Living in this manner, without control over one's life, and direction, is potentially damaging.

Satan tempts us into a relationship that seems pure; however as each day passes, we may get to be more emotionally and physically involved. We may reach a point of being unable to handle the consequences.

Keep in mind that when you let someone enter your heart and soul, the relationship will become a very intimate experience. You may even become dependent on that relationship and that person's constant presence in your life. The other person will share herself, or himself, with you and your existence.

If we think clearly and plainly – disregarding the illusion of dating – we may then ask ourselves: "How did I get to this point?" Days and months pass, and you may find yourself entangled with many difficult issues stemming from that relationship. The bond becomes an imprint on your heart that cannot easily be forgotten in a week, a month, and unfortunately sometimes years.

Hanging Out

If you start talking with someone, and you feel comfortable with that person, you will tend to try to find opportunities to be with that person. It is still while you are in a group, and not on a one-to-one basis. "There is nothing wrong with talking to someone who is nice and attractive. I am just hanging out, and simply having a good time, but not dating," you may say. We need to be always mindful of our motives behind our interest? Are there certain desires that are not as clear, or not so innocent in that relationship? Is there an honest and sincere friendship that is budding? Are you at a maturity stage, where you want to explore your options with that person, for possible lifelong commitment?

Irrespective what people may call these outings; ask yourself if your time with this person is pure and acceptable to God.

Is his or her appearance stirring up emotions that may not be so pure? If your emotions and thoughts are pure and sincere, does this hold true for the other person also? What are your expectations from that relationship? To keep yourself in check, you need to ask yourself: "Can the Lord, the Holy One, be present with me when I am hanging out with that individual, even while I am in a group of people? Will He be pleased with every action, thought, and intention?"

This is a very serious matter, and we truly need to be honest, straightforward, and crystal clear with ourselves. As Christians, we always need to evaluate our behaviors, thoughts, and even our deepest intentions, in the light of the words of God. We will be held responsible in front of the Almighty, our heavenly Father.

I Am Not Odd

People think that if the majority is dating then they should be as well; otherwise, they would be perceived as strange or old fashioned. Our society states that if you are good-looking and sociable – you should be dating. If you are not, then there's something wrong with you.

You are not going to be less experienced in life if you do not date. You are not going to be odd, if you don't regularly hang out with someone of the opposite sex. We should not be quick to entertain society's expectations. Some women believe that there is something intrinsically wrong with them, if they are not asked out. With disappointment, they over-analyze why that may be the case, often reaching erroneous conclusions. Their self-esteem suffers, and they begin to act differently. They change the way they talk, behave, and dress in order to attract men's attention. Likewise, men may experience an insult to their self-esteem, if women do not react to them as they hope.

Remember that you are whole and complete in yourself through your relationship with the Lord. God created you, and He loves you. Accept yourself and live your life to please Him and glorify His name. By focusing on the Lord, He will surely open our eyes, enlighten our minds and show us the right people with whom we will interact.

Patricia and Peter

Patricia, 20, was talking to Maria about her friend, Peter, 24. He lived in California, and she lived in New York. She met him on a church trip to Los Angeles. Since then, they kept in touch by email and telephone. He even visited her in New York several times. She always felt unsettled. Patricia was not too crazy about Peter, but he was very charming and persuasive. He succeeded in convincing her that he truly loved her. Finally, after six months of his charm, she began to have feelings for him.

While visiting him on a second trip to Los Angeles, she became convinced that he was in fact "the one." Their relationship became more intimate. However, a month after she returned home, he called and broke up with her! She was shocked and hurt. She even blamed herself for not showing him love earlier, or that she might have been rude and inconsiderate.

One year later, Peter called her wanting to get back together! He apologized for that day when he broke up with her. He explained that he was drunk at the time, and was not aware of what he was saying. He said he made a mistake. Wisely, Patricia utterly rejected his explanations.

The truth turned out to be that there was another girl in his life at the same time he was seeing Patricia. She was left hanging there, in case he broke up with the other girl. Peter did indeed break up with the second girl, and that was why he tried to return to Patricia.

In this scenario, one individual manipulated someone else's feelings (and life), to ensure their personal satisfaction and "happiness." This non-Christian demeanor is obviously selfish, and not Biblically or socially acceptable.

Are you Serious?

If you are not at a stage of intellectual, psychological, emotional and spiritual maturity to make serious, lifelong decisions, then going out on a one-to-one basis should be deferred for a later, more appropriate time. Seeing someone on a one-to-one basis needs to be reserved for when one is contemplating marriage. It is most appropriate, and to your best interest, to go out in groups – thus avoiding being alone with a particular person. By going out in groups, you will also prevent the potential slip to damaging consequences. Interact with the group as a whole, not separating yourselves from them (e.g. talking romantically together on the side).

If you are contemplating marriage, it is better to start getting to know that person properly in a group setting. You can observe the way she/he talks and behaves in different situations. You can get to know her/him at get-togethers, trips, retreats, church, work, school, Bible study groups, and at other places and circumstances – still within a group setting. Pray that God may guide you, and show you the qualities of that person. (More to be discussed in later chapters)

If after your careful observations, diligent prayer, guidance, and circumspect thinking, you conclude that pursuing a relationship – for a future together – is the right decision, then it is appropriate to express your interest to her. (At this point, it is important to mention that both, the man and the woman, should let their families, and spiritual fathers/advisors, know of their involvement. They will guide them and pray for them. Their families/advisors can be excellent accountability sources, to keep their relationship on the right track).

Use of Time

One ends up investing a lot of time, energy and emotions in dating. The time you think about going out, getting ready, and actually meeting the person takes many hours. You may then reminisce about all the things you had talked about, and then spend a lot of time telling a close friend all that had happened. Afterwards, you may start planning for the next time you will see each other, and so on.

How would one feel, if after six months of a relationship (aimed at just a friendship), they are told by the other individual, "I want to end this relationship." Be mindful that this ending could be without any clear explanation. Sometimes, people terminate their relationship abruptly, without a clear communication of the reasons. Will you consider this time in your life as an experience you went through? That period of time was more of harm to you – spiritually and emotionally. In addition, you might not have used your time productively.

On the other hand, when you have attained a stage of maturity, and you are serious about that relationship, you will be more likely to use your time vigilantly and wisely. You will be aiming at a future with the other individual. On the contrary, the non-serious relationship was just aimed at "hanging out." It was merely spending time with someone – without a clear and pure goal, and mostly ending with problems. Instead of expending our energies on dating, let's find a more beneficial use of our time, until we are ready.

Do not forget that a minute that passes cannot be lived again. It becomes a memory, and is gone forever. Let us invest our time wisely. We can participate in activities that build our psychological, emotional and spiritual well-being – to edify ourselves, as well as others. We can use our time to read, pray, meditate, serve our families and enjoy life in a godly way. We can go out of our way to help family members, the needy, and those who do not have anyone to remember them. We can go on trips, go camping, excel in sports, revive old friendships, and serve in Church. There are endless wonderful opportunities for the use of our time. Use your time in the best possible way to grow spiritually, and understand what the Lord wants from you.

Conclusion

People who date may often start a relationship based on selfish reasons. At times, the relationship takes a detour for the worse, causing much emotional and spiritual harm to those involved.

From the story of Patricia and Peter, we observed how one could play with another's feelings. Peter's goal was not right from the beginning. If we carefully trace back to a time prior to the couple getting involved, we will find that Peter had the mindset that many people may have toward dating and relationships: "It's just a very close friendship, and there is no harm being done. If it does not work out, I will find someone else. At least I have had a good time."

As we saw in their story, and as we will see in the stories to come, dating is a very slippery road that may have serious consequences that should not be overlooked. Do your best to evaluate your life, friendships, and how you spend your time.

We need to think of where the path is taking us, and

not to be swayed by the pressures of society and the media.

May the Holy Spirit continue to work in you to live a true Christian life.

"Let no one despise your youth, but be an example to the believers in word, in conduct, in love, in spirit, in faith, in purity" (1 Timothy 4:12).

6

Dating a Non-Christian

In the previous chapter, we discussed how dating is a very slippery road. In this chapter, we will explore the topic of dating a non-Christian. We need to know the various issues and consequences accompanying dating a non-Christian. Let us study what the Bible mentions about a similar condition in 1 Kings 11.

"But King Solomon loved many foreign women… from the nations of whom the LORD had said to the children of Israel, 'You shall not intermarry with them, nor they with you. Surely they will turn away your hearts after their gods.' Solomon clung to these in love" (v.1-2).

"For it was so, when Solomon was old, that his wives turned his heart after other gods; and his heart was not loyal to the LORD his God, as *was* the heart of his father David. For Solomon went after Ashtoreth the goddess of the Sidonians, and after Milcom the abomination of the Ammonites" (v.4-5).

"Solomon did evil in the sight of the LORD, and did not fully follow the LORD, as *did* his father David" (v.6).

"So the LORD became angry with Solomon, because his heart had turned from the LORD God of Israel, who had appeared to him twice" (v.9).

"Therefore the LORD said to Solomon, 'Because you have done this, and have not kept My covenant and My statutes, which I have commanded you, I will surely tear the kingdom away from you and give it to your servant' "v.11).

King Solomon married many foreign women who were not Israelites. They were from nations that God had told them not to intermarry, yet King Solomon married many women from these nations, and clung to his foreign wives in love. He did not keep the covenant and statutes of God. Although the Lord had clearly stated that his heart would be turned away from Him, still, King Solomon clung to them in love. It is surprising that King Solomon, with all his wisdom and power, turned away from God, who had appeared to him twice.

God Almighty knows our weaknesses and where we may get tempted. Solomon let himself drift and, little by little, the commandments might have been forgotten, become not practical, or even far-fetched. Could it be that his wealth and wisdom gave him a sense of security and power? We are not sure, but the Bible did mention that he disobeyed God who gave him all the wisdom, riches and honor.

An Emotional Trap

The foreign women in King Solomon's story symbolize any non-Christian person whom we are considering to be involved with in a relationship, or even marry. Subsequently, we may well be in the same situation as King Solomon – in that our hearts will be turned away from God. Someone may then ask: "If King Solomon with all his power and wealth fell, are we stronger or wiser than him? Are we immune from falling?" The answer is that we are not. We wish that such immunity did exist in order to prevent many mistakes, falls and heartaches; and to allow us to live holy for the Lord.

If you think about it, Satan will not present us with an ugly, or less than average person. Instead, a handsome man or a beautiful woman, who may be a non-Christian, will come our way. We convince ourselves that he or she is perfect in every *other* aspect, except when it comes to their religion, or spirituality. You then start compromising: "Maybe if I go out with him once, I will see if he is truly that good of a person, or not." You start spending time together and growing closer. At this point, the thought of breaking up is further removed from your mind and you rationalize: "Surely, since we like each other, things could be worked out. It is not fair that, just for religion's sake, we cannot be together." You may even add, "Although spirituality is lacking, I may witness to him, and win him for Christ. After all, isn't that what Christianity tells us to do? God is love, and He does not want anyone to be lost, and maybe He wants me to bring him to Christianity. I can do all things through Christ who strengthens me."

Practically, it is almost impossible to witness to him about the Lord, and see how he is progressing spiritually, without getting emotionally involved. And if it happens that you get emotionally involved, will you find yourself trapped in a situation with many ramifications that you may not know how to undo? This whole scenario may become even more complicated if you get physically involved.

After you are emotionally invested, you will probably wonder, "If he is unwilling to convert to Christianity, and I continue with him; I may lose my spirituality, and maybe my eternity. But if I leave him and choose God, I will get hurt, and I may never meet someone like him again. I love him, and he is a great person." The more time goes by, the more you may become spiritually cold, and your discernment to what is right or wrong gets blurred and unclear. Even though you may think that you are rationalizing correctly, you may not be thinking clearly enough. Finally, your decision to leave him, or not, may end up being an emotional one, and not a spiritually-oriented decision.

Watch this slippery road and seek guidance. Your faith and your commitment to the Lord need to be strong. You do not need to be dragged down a dead end alley, with all its temptations and sins.

Will You Marry Him?

Now we come to other points that you will need to think about, if you are planning to tread on this road. First of all, if you are intending to marry him, which Church will accept to celebrate the Sacrament of Matrimony between a Christian and a non-Christian? What will you do if you do not find a Church that will accept it? When it comes to your families, will you involve them in the process? What will their reactions be toward that relationship? In case they disagree with you, will you separate yourselves from both families?

Let us also consider his situation. Will he accept to attend church with you? What about if you are planning to have kids, will they grow up as Christians? Will he agree to take them to church? Will he respect that you may want to fast and pray? Will he fast and pray with you?

When it comes to reading the Bible, will you read together or will you live separate spiritual lives? Take note that he may accept all or some of what you are asking now, but later he may very well change his mind.

These are just a few of the many questions you need to address before venturing into this life. The best advice in these situations is to avoid the "Good Samaritan attitude." That mind-set is one of the ways Satan lures us into his snares. Others' experiences show us that this is a dangerous path. The chances that you will slip far exceed the chances that you will win him over. So why play with fire?

> "For how do you know, O wife, whether you will save *your* husband? Or how do you know, O husband, whether you will save *your* wife?" (1 Corinthians 7:16).

What you can do is pray for that person, because prayers can do miracles. Let him meet your priest or pastor, or any of the Church's spiritual leaders who can guide him in the right path. If he really wants to know the Lord, He will reveal Himself to him. "If anyone wills to do His will, he shall know concerning the doctrine, whether it is from God or *whether* I speak on My own *authority*" (John 7:17).

Be watchful of where situations like these can take you. Get support from people who really love you, and can guide you in the light of God's words. The Lord can never let you down, since you have His promise in His son.

Unequally Yoked

> Kim, 23, was in her last year of college. She had been going out with a Christian man when she began to lose sight of her relationship with God. She eventually broke up with him, and began "dating" a non-Christian doctor. Her heart grew even colder toward God. She was very intimate in her relationship, and she was sexually involved. Within four months they were married (civil marriage). Their marriage was shaky, as they had many disagreements and arguments.

The Lord, the Light, did not exist in her first relationship, and also in her marriage. God was not asked to be involved. It was an earthly and lustful relationship from the beginning. They were divorced in less than a year! Her heart was hardened and she became bitter. Several church friends had tried to talk with her to save her from her misery, but she turned them away. She ended up suffering from severe depression, for which she needed to see a psychiatrist.

In 2 Corinthians 6:14-16, we read, "Do not be unequally yoked together with unbelievers. For what fellowship has righteousness with lawlessness? And what communion has light with darkness? And what accord has Christ with Belial? Or what part has a believer with an unbeliever? And what agreement has the temple of God with idols? For you are the temple of the living God. As God has said: '*I will dwell in them And walk among them. I will be their God, And they shall be My people.*'"

In the farms, the yoke is a wooden bar or frame by which two oxen (or other animals) are joined at the heads or necks. It allows them to work together. The farmers use the yoke when they want the animals to carry certain things together, or in farming the land. There is "togetherness"; in the same path; without separation; carrying burdens; and supporting each other. The same applies to humans. St. Paul was giving this analogy to illustrate that believers can not be "yoked" with unbelievers. It is an inequality in the connection and load – a disharmony of the relationship.

Now, let's look at this problem from another perspective. Marriage is a union of two bodies, souls and spirits. However, God was not present in Kim's marriage; hers was merely a union of two bodies, partially of two souls, and no union of their spirits. The spiritual aspect, which is the one intended by God to regulate the physical and emotional aspects, did not exist at all. There was a huge hollow defect in that marriage. This situation resulted in an unbalanced and unfruitful union, with many problems that could not be solved. Divorce, which is yet another devastation, was unfortunately inevitable.

Diana and Dean

Diana, 24, was from a devout Christian family. She had finished college two years earlier and had moved out of her parents' house. She stayed with a girlfriend she had known since high school. However, she moved back home when she ran into financial troubles. She had been "dating" Dean, 28, an atheist, for the previous four months.

One day, Diana paged her friend, Lauren, with a 911 code at 1:00 am. Diana was crying hysterically, saying, "I have really messed up!" They decided to meet at the church at that very hour. The church was closed, so they sat on the stairs, and she began to describe her situation to Lauren.

Diana explained that she had met Dean at one of her friends' parties, four months earlier.

From their first encounter, they just "clicked." They started talking and soon, they were dating. She liked many attributes in Dean's personality. Then, with a sobbing and a grief-stricken voice she said, "We had sex. I'm afraid that I might be pregnant!" She went on to say that her friend was an atheist. Lauren tried to calm her, being as compassionate as she could. Diana continued, and said that the relationship evolved very quickly, and she had become very attached to him. In time, their relationship became very intimate. They became physically involved, and eventually had sex.

She blamed herself for this ordeal, and could not stop crying. She was terrified of the possibility that she might be pregnant. She was also scared to death of anyone finding out – especially her parents, who are devout Christians. Lauren prayed with her, and promised to be supportive, and took her back home.

Later, Diana went to church and spoke with a priest about her mistakes. She then started attending services and meetings regularly. She seemed to be on the right track once again. However, a few weeks later, Lauren noticed that Diana was avoiding her. She suspected that something was going on between her and Dean again. When Lauren inquired as to what was going on, Diana replied that everything was fine, and that she did not need the Church anymore. Lauren sensed the denial in her voice. Later, Diana admitted that, in fact, she had never broken up with Dean! She actually moved in with him. She explained the situation to her parents, who were initially outraged, but then felt tremendously guilty. Her parents blamed themselves, and thought that if they had raised her well, she would not have gone astray. At the same time, they also could not prevent her from leaving the house. They did not want to lose contact with her, and wanted to let her know that they still loved her. They told her she could come back home at anytime.

They prayed and fasted for her, and they asked some of her Christian friends to pray for her as well, and to keep in touch with her. She was a lost sheep, and the Good Shepherd will not leave her to the world.

Diana stayed with him out of shame. "I did it with him, so now I have to stay with him; or else I would be like a prostitute! If, in the future, I marry anyone else, I will always remember that I had a relationship with Dean, and I will never feel comfortable." Diana was trying to rationalize what some people consider as "suffering for love." She lost her virginity, and she was considering the pain she was in as a type of suffering she had to endure for this "love." This concept shows that Diana had a distorted image of true love.

Love is not physical or biological. Diana and Dean mistakenly labeled the chemistry between them, as love; but actually it was lust. Many men and women make a similar mistake when they conclude that when they "click," this must mean that they are "in love." With that "click," the individuals will start daydreaming about each other, and will be living in a fantasy. That click could have been merely from sharing a few things in common at that moment, without having matching personalities.

True love, on the contrary, is what is written in 1 Corinthians 13 with its sincerity, honesty, selflessness and spirituality.

Conclusion

As St. Paul mentioned, there is no fellowship between righteousness and lawlessness. There is no communion between light and darkness. You need to know that dating a non-Christian is not the right path our Lord and Savior Jesus Christ intended us to tread on.

Furthermore, we will not be conducting our lives according to His commandments, and we will be facing many problems. Also, as we learn from the experiences of others, the outcomes of these relationships are far more grievous. If you are interested in someone who is not a Christian, be cognizant of where this road will lead you. Do not let the days pass unnoticed, and discover too late that you are so attached to that person. You may end up sharing your life with him out of personal dependence and convenience. Prevention is better than treatment. It is better to avoid the situation altogether than getting trapped.

On the other hand, if the other individual is willing to convert to Christianity, then this is a totally different scenario. Still, this relationship has its risks. You need to involve the Church, your family, and friends. Guidance is a must in such situations. You need to tread on this road very cautiously, with wise discernment, and unceasing prayers.

"Who *is* wise and understanding among you? Let him show by good conduct *that* his works *are done* in the meekness of wisdom" (James 3:13).

7

Cohabitation

In the 1970's, it was considered illegal in the United States for a man and woman to live together without being married. Times have changed, and people's habits, ideals and convictions have changed. Many people are misled, and think that the commandments of God are neither applicable nor practical to the 21st century. Now, more and more couples are choosing to live together for various reasons. Some people feel a certain thrill by living with their partner without being married to them. That thrill paves the way for more and more mistakes and sins.

"Most people now live together before they marry for the first time. An even higher percentage of those divorced who subsequently remarry live together first. And a growing number of persons, both young and old, are living together with no plans for eventual marriage." [1]

"Between 1960 and 2004, the number of unmarried couples in America increased by nearly 1200 *(twelve hundred)* percent. It is estimated that about a quarter of unmarried women age 25 to 39 are currently living with a partner and an additional quarter have lived with a partner at some time in the past. Over half of all first marriages are now preceded by living together, compared to virtually none 50 years ago." [1]

"Recent data show that among women in the 19-44 age range, 60 percent of high school dropouts have cohabited compared to 37 percent of college graduates. Cohabitation is also more common among those who are less religious than their peers, those who have been divorced, and those who have experienced parental divorce, fatherlessness, or high levels of marital discord during childhood. A growing percentage of cohabiting couple households, now over 40 percent, contains children." [1]

Those who cohabitate, try to rationalize their beliefs, offering various excuses explaining their decisions. Also, they downplay the gravity of their ill decision and their consequences – which are often quite devastating. As Christians, to cohabitate is to disobey our heavenly Father. It is a sinful road.

Some may not recognize a difference between marriage, and living together. They think, "What's the difference? We are going to live together either way. The difference is just a piece of paper – a marriage certificate." They may even completely forgo the whole idea of marriage.

> Annette, 25, was living with Gary, 27, who was not a Christian. She said, "Initially, I thought of living with Gary as a wonderful opportunity, but later I discovered the misery and wretchedness of my life. I thought that we were very much alike in many ways, and we communicated well. I lived with him for three years before we decided to get married (civil marriage). I knew that I was doing something wrong, but I kept treading on that path, not sure of where I was going. Deep inside me though, I had an uncomfortable feeling.
>
> Soon after we got married, everything fell apart. We discovered that each one of us was living in a silo. The independence, each one had, could not be found anymore. Arguments and fights were our daily routine.
>
> This marriage was not blessed by my heavenly Father,

and I was reaping what I sowed."

Annette thought she was following a path that would make her happy yet; she never attained a glimpse of what she had hoped.

Ask yourself

If you are living with someone, or considering it, ask yourself these questions:

- Will you be able to participate in church services and activities, or will you feel uncomfortable attending?
- What will happen if you come across words in the Bible that reprimand the way you are living?
- Will you try to interpret certain Bible verses to suit your situation?
- How do you see what you are doing in the eyes of the Creator?
- What about if you had kids? How are you going to rear them? Will they be Christians?
- Consider your family and friends. Will you feel accepted or rejected by them, or will you isolate yourself?
- Will you move out of your neighborhood – to one that is more liberal?
- What will happen if you break up with your partner?
- Will you feel the need to find someone else to live with, or will you re-evaluate your ways in light of the word of God, and try to change your way of life?
- Will cohabiting offer you a "smooth exit" if things don't work out?

- What if you return home and don't find your partner. Since you don't have a commitment, anyone can opt out at anytime. Will the fear of not finding your partner be haunting you whenever you are away from each other – especially after you had a disagreement? Will you then act subserviently so that your partner prefers you and doesn't leave you for someone else?
- Without marital vows blessed by the Lord, you are offering a green light to your partner to cheat on you. And if he does, will you offer him the excuse that you were not married? This does not mean that those who are married in Church do not experience infidelities. They do, and we hear about them. However, the percentage of loyalty, in a blessed union by the Lord, far exceeds the infidelity. On the other hand, the percentage of infidelity, in a non-Church marriage, far exceeds the loyalty to each other.

These are just a few questions to help you consider this matter before venturing down that road. Don't risk subjecting yourself to circumstances and occurrences. Instead, try to answer the questions in a rational, honest and godly way while reconsidering your situation.

Possible Excuses for Cohabitation

1. Fear of commitment

The fear of the lifelong commitment of marriage, and its responsibilities, leads people to opt for cohabitation. This fear is also compounded by a fear of divorce. However, breaking up after living with someone will result in the exact same feelings, and agony, that married couples experience after a divorce.

2. Sex

Sex becomes conveniently available when a couple cohabitates. There is now no need to search for it anymore; and for some, no need to get married either.

> Lucy, 35, had been living with her boyfriend for nearly a year. One time she said something very sad: "I make him happy (sexually) and he makes me happy. What else do I need?"

This belief is based on sensualities and the misconception of what happiness means. There are certainly more important things to life than lustful physical satisfaction.

3. Running away

Some may be attempting to escape from a broken family. Others may be living with an alcoholic, drug addicted, or abusive parent. This situation is dangerous because these desperate individuals may just go out with whoever is available for them. In effect, they try to solve one problem at home with another problem.

Leslie, 21, had not seen her father for years, since her parents divorced. She had felt unloved, and she sought love by moving in with her boyfriend. He was unemployed and he abused her. Her family tried to persuade her to return, but she refused. She claimed that she was in love with him. Was that really true love? Leslie did not really know where she was heading. If she were asked about her situation, it would be unlikely for her to answer clearly and confidently.

She sought love that would have filled her heart, as a substitute, she found a physical relationship that offered her more emptiness. Over time, she lost the peace, joy and energy that she used to have.

4. Experimenting for marriage

Rose, 27, decided to move in with Ted, 29, and claimed, "We love each other and we need to know for sure if we are meant for each other, and if we can get along."

She made living together sound like a laboratory project, or experiment. Should one experiment with fornication and adultery? Will God bless this relationship? What are the criteria you will use to then go ahead with marriage? Will there be a deadline at which you will finally decide what you are going to do? (Even if a couple sets a deadline, the chances are that they will keep postponing it – offering that they are not yet ready and that they need more time).

This idea of experimenting for marriage is an illusion – having no basis – and we should not be entrapped by it. Living together does not prevent future mistakes nor increase one's chances of having a successful marriage – quite the opposite. One report in the United States found that unmarried cohabitations, overall, are less stable than marriages. The probability of a first marriage ending in a separation or divorce within 5 years is 20%, but the probability of a premarital cohabitation breaking up within 5 years is 49%. After 10 years, the probability of a first marriage ending is 33%, compared with 62% for cohabitations.[2]

As you can see, the rationalizations that some people offer that allow them to experiment with cohabitation are not well thought out. They are mainly geared toward satisfying certain lustful desires.

5. To save money

Laura, 24, had been living with Jack, 25, for 4 months. Although both of them came from wealthy families, they claimed that they wanted to save money for the wedding, their future and for the kids! Their reasoning was distorted by their desires to live together.

6. Not understanding marriage

Marriage, being created by God, is not well understood by many couples. There is a very special joy in marriage. It is not just a ceremony sealed with a signed set of papers. It is a sacrament where the Holy Spirit dwells and works in the hearts and lives of the couple. If couples really understood the value and joy of marriage, they would likely choose to save themselves for their future spouse. They would decide to avoid the risks and sins associated with cohabitation.

Finally, let us bring to mind a few Bible verses to help us live in holiness, glorifying His name:

"and have put on the new *man* who is renewed in knowledge
according to the
image of Him who created him"
(Colossians 3:10).

"For this is the will of God, your sanctification:
that you should abstain from sexual immorality"
(1 Thessalonians 4:3).

"But God did not call us to uncleanness,
but in holiness"
(1 Thessalonians 4:7).

"Flee also youthful lusts; but pursue righteousness, faith, love,
peace with those who call
on the Lord out of a pure heart"
(2 Timothy 2:22).

Notes

1. The National Marriage Project, Rutgers, The State University of New Jersey, co-directed by David Popenoe, Ph.D., and Barbara Dafoe Whitehead, Ph.D. (2005). Used with permission.

2. (CDC Series Report 23, Number 22. 103pp. (PHS) 98-1998). http://www.cdc.gov/nchs/data/series/sr_23/sr23_022.pdf

8

Premarital Sex

> "But I say to you that whoever looks at a
> woman to lust for her has already
> committed adultery with her in his heart"
> (Matthew 5:28).

The media can strongly affect our thoughts and values, and ultimately, our decision-making process. Television, movies, advertising, and popular music continually promote sexual behavior in general and premarital sex in particular. Singers and songwriters openly express their liberal views of sex, and impose their beliefs on listeners. We are constantly bombarded by sexual images all around us. Just observe magazines at any newsstand or supermarket checkout line, and you will find it almost impossible to avoid graphic, sexual images.

Men and women are constantly surrounded by misleading views from the media – twenty-four hours a day, seven days a week. As a result, people are confused and swayed by the state of beliefs around them. It gets more and more difficult to differentiate between right and wrong – often believing that what's "right" can vary, depend on the situation, subject to modification, and is by no means objective or universal.

What has developed is the misconception that sex is not that big of a deal. Our society says, "If it feels good do not deprive yourself; on the contrary, go ahead and express those desires and emotions." These ideals have taken root, and born fruit, in the secular world – so much so that some shamelessly brag about their sexual experiences!

Furthermore, this concept of sex leads people to slip into and out of short-term relationships, not moving toward the goal of a lifelong commitment through the Sacrament of Matrimony. If an individual does not find satisfaction in a sexual relationship, he will jump to another. Ultimately, dating may merely become a transient sexual "entertainment," where a person can change partners as easily as he changes channels on a television.

On the other hand, someone may say: "I have been having sex with my girlfriend for several years now, and I have no desire to jump from this relationship to another. I am totally committed to her." This situation also, when lacking the blessed union of the Sacrament of Matrimony, is not in accordance with the Lord and His commandments.

Intimacy, Love and Sex

True intimacy comes from love, respect and commitment (as described in 1 Corinthians 13). The only place to share an intimate relationship with the opposite sex is in the lifelong commitment of marriage. However, many people will not wait for marriage, and seek sexual intimacy in premarital relationships. This problem is then compounded when these physical relations, built on lust and sins, are misconstrued for true intimacy.

People confuse the intensity of romance and sex, with the intimacy of love. Love is a process; sex is an act within a process. Love takes time to mature and develop, while sex is instinctive. Love deepens a relationship; sex, without love, respect and commitment, drains a relationship. Love and sex in marriage are sacred, while premarital sex will offer nothing but false love, fear, shame, heartache, sins, and more. The cumulative factors of the sexual activities will certainly create a shallow, irritable, sensual and selfish person, whose whole being will be damaged.

Can you imagine what your marriage would be like if sex was the main bond that connected you with your future husband/wife? Would your marriage fall apart if, after some time, the sexual desire is not as inflamed as it was originally? The level of excitement you used to have before marriage is not there any more.

Alternatively, intimacy and commitment in marriage will create an environment for sexual fulfillment, not the other way around. Do not forget that God Himself is love, and every other love is contained within the sphere of His love.

If our focus and goals are right, then our intentions, desires, and paths need to be right as well. True love, based on living according to the commandments of God, will enrich our lives, and will place us on the right track in life. On the other hand, seeking lusts and momentary pleasures will ruin our lives.

Sin is packaged very appealingly in our society – it comes with a promise of immediate satisfaction and pleasure, and lures people downhill until it ensnares them. "Therefore we also, since we are surrounded by so great a cloud of witnesses, let us lay aside every weight, and the sin which so easily ensnares *us,* and let us run with endurance the race that is set before us" (Hebrews 12:1).

Possible Reasons for Engaging in Premarital Sex

Amidst unsteady values, unclear and insufficient

direction, and lack of spiritual fervor, people will tend to submit to sensual desires and temptations. What will follow, are rationalizations offered as excuses for inappropriate actions.

Let us enumerate some of the reasons and misconceptions why individuals engage in sex (keep in mind that the use of alcohol and drugs will lower inhibition and self-control):

- "If you love your partner, it is OK."
- "Everyone else is doing it."
- "Sex is simply a necessary part of intimacy."
- "There is no harm done – as long as you use protection."
- "You simply must experience it."
- "You will be missing out."
- "It is thrilling, and it feels good."
- "As long as it is consensual, it is OK."
- "There's too much pressure on me; I need to get it over with."
- "We're going to get married anyway."

For many people, romance and "love" are the greatest determining factors in deciding whether or not to engage in sex. Unfortunately, these often take precedence over the importance and sanctity of the Sacrament of Matrimony, the consequences of premarital sex, and the couple's reputation.

> There was once an engaged couple who convinced themselves that premarital sex was fine. They thought, since they loved each other and they would be married in several months, becoming sexually active was no harm. Instead of getting a jumpstart on what would be holy relations in the context of their future marriage, they had to bear the guilt and shame of their act. The Holy Spirit had awakened their conscience to realize what they had done.

Our Lord Jesus Christ spoke of the Holy Spirit saying, "And when He has come, He will convict the world of sin, and of righteousness, and of judgment" (John 16:8). The Holy Spirit convicts us of our sins so that we may return to the Father. We need to listen to Him and follow His guidance to our lives.

Consequences of Premarital Sex

Besides sin, the following could be some of the consequences of premarital sex:

1. Loss of virginity
2. Pregnancy
3. Forced marriage
4. STDs
5. Emotional distress
6. Guilt and shame
7. Tainted self-image and self-hatred
8. Feelings of failure and loss of hope
9. Sexual addiction
10. Abortion
11. Adoption
12. Unintended Parenthood
13. Alcohol and drug abuse
14. Deteriorating family relationships
15. Job loss or academic failure
16. Further spiritual alienation
17. Becoming a stumbling block to those who may follow your example
18. Loss of respect of your future spouse
19. Comparing your future spouse to past relationships

20. Being compared to your spouse's past relationships

Premarital sex could be a very horrifying experience, and not at all an emotionally satisfying one, as some people imagine. It is capable of creating a terrible guilt, and a feeling of being exposed and demoralized. Premarital sex can leave a permanent stain on an individual, and can make one feel like a used object.

Although premarital sex could be a major factor in breaking up a relationship, it may also create a false sense of attachment. It makes it difficult for the couple to recognize other factors meriting separation. The couple may continue this "convenient" relationship, while violating God's commandments. Eventually, this situation can cause one to feel stressed, trapped, used and guilty.

Others, despite the fact of knowing it is a sin, continue in the relationship. They may break up for sometime, and then they may get back to each other. They may keep on vacillating between being together for sometime, and breaking up. When the guilt is strong and the voice of the Lord, blaming them, is clear, they break up. Then, after sometime, they may become less fervent spiritually, and they start longing for each other. They end up being together again. This swinging relationship needs true and faithful repentant individuals, not wavering to the traps of the devil or the self. Let's discuss a couple of the consequences of premarital sex in detail.

Comparisons from the past

Sharon, 29, said she would never want to compare her future husband to anyone else, nor would she want him to compare her to any of his former relationships. She does not want to have memories of her wrongdoings after she gets married.

She met Robert, 34, who told her that he had been with several women before meeting her. Despite this confession, he was still able to win over her heart, and she became very much attached to him. Soon enough, they were engaged. Down the road, the details of his past started to bother her. She felt that he still had a lingering attachment to his past, especially when his past relationships came up in conversation. She thought to herself: "He is a nice man and I'm sure many women would love to be with him, but how do I know that he will not cheat on me? If he is still attached to his past without being repentant about his previous relations, the chances are that he will have an extramarital affair. Will I be able to live in constant doubt? Will I be constantly trying to please him so that he doesn't leave me for another woman? Will I always be jealous? Why didn't he marry one of those women, and why does he now choose me to be his wife? Will he compare me with anyone of them? I do not know if his heart is still intact to be wholly with me. I may always feel that I am not special in his eyes. What if, one day, he calls me by one of their names? Why should I give him my best – my heart – while he is giving me one that has been torn to pieces?"

Sharon could not stand all these doubts and questions. She prayed diligently and sought spiritual guidance. After a great deal of struggle, she finally broke up the engagement with Robert.

This does not mean that everyone who has had previous relations will always get rejected and never get married. However, unless the person has repented, showed a positive attitude toward changing his life, and is living for the Lord, it could be anticipated that he may repeat his behavior. Sharon could have accepted Robert had he been repentant, and had not been so attached to his past experiences.

Soon afterwards, she doubted whether she had made the right decision in leaving him. She was tempted to return to him. She felt lonely, depressed, heartbroken, and could not function properly at work, or at home. She tried to engage herself in different activities to get her mind off him, and to go on with her life. She found support in her friends, family, prayer, meditation and her spiritual father.

After quite some time, she slowly felt relieved and freed from those taunting and oppressive feelings. She was back to her active and lively self once again. She is waiting on God who will guide her to *discover* the right person for her. She wants to enjoy life – to its maximum – in a happy, blessed and pure relationship.

Can you imagine someone, having a history of premarital sex (and the baggage accompanying those experiences), unrepentantly kneeling in front of the altar on his wedding day, and telling his spouse, "I am not a virgin, and you are not as special in my eyes as you may have thought?" There is a joy in being the one – the only one – for the other. Giving your heart completely to God, and the person with whom you will share the rest of your life, is an inexpressible joy.

Sexual addiction

Some people perceive sex as a basic need, and therefore will do whatever it takes to get it. They think that if they abstain from sex for too long, they will not be able to function properly. Other individuals believe that having sex will relieve sexual tension, and lower their desire, but what will happen is the opposite. Seeking sexual satisfaction becomes an addiction that consumes their very existence. They want it; and without it, they are not able to function. It becomes like a drug that consumes them. As time goes on, they want more and more of that drug. They may feel the need to increase the "dosage" of sex in order to reach satisfaction. Premarital sex can create an intense desire for more sex that can never be quenched, leading to sexual addiction and promiscuity. This vicious cycle can eventually destroy the person.

This type of existence is degrading and shameful to the human race, which was created in the image of God. He created us to live a life of honor, dignity and glory – with Him, and for Him.

If we look at the heart of the problem, we will find that it is spiritual emptiness. Sex-preoccupied individuals desperately seek to fill this emptiness by satiating their physical lusts. However, they often get caught in the trap of sexual addiction. Our search for complete satisfaction would ultimately lead us to God. We are completely satisfied when we are united with Him. Nothing, and no one, can fill our spiritual emptiness except our God and Savior Jesus Christ.

The problem occurs when we misdirect our search from godly joy and peace, to self-centered desires that can only give a *false* sense of satisfaction. St. Augustine confessed to God, "You have made us for Yourself, and our hearts are restless until we find rest in You."

Another reason why some individuals find themselves constantly seeking sexual relationships is an attempt to feel loved. This search can throw them into a destructive and immoral cycle that is never gratifying or fulfilling.

> Eileen, 19, was from a God-fearing family. She was the youngest of three. Her parents tried their best to raise her in a godly environment. They used to take her to church every Sunday, and brought her to Sunday school. As she grew up, the care and attention that she had received as a child decreased. She started looking for that attention, or as she put it "love," somewhere else – mainly form her male friends whom she started dating.

The men she dated abused her sexually. Despite her hurt, she felt "loved," even for a short time. She did not find love or attention at home. Those momentary lustful pleasures, with all the shame and guilt they produced, were important for her to feel loved and cared for by someone. Sexual pleasure became an addiction that consumed her life.

Date Rape and Sexual Assault

It is important to mention a few things about date rape (or "drug-facilitated sexual assault") and drinking parties. The main focus of the assailants is to indulge in their sexual and sensual fantasies at the expense of someone else. Date rapes and drinking parties are on the rise on college campuses. More than half of all rapes on women occur before age 19.

Drugs, like rohypnol ("roofies"), gamma-hydroxybutyric acid (GHB), and ketamine, are a few of the drugs used by perpetrators. We need to mention few points about rohypnol and GHB.

> Rohypnol and GHB are predominantly central nervous system depressants. Since they are often colorless, tasteless, and odorless, they can be added to beverages and ingested unknowingly.

> Rohypnol, a trade name for flunitrazepam, belongs to a class of drugs known as benzodiazepines. Rohypnol can incapacitate victims and prevent them from resisting sexual assault. It can produce "anterograde amnesia," which means individuals may not remember events they experienced while under the effects of the drug. Also, Rohypnol may be lethal when mixed with alcohol and/or other depressants. Rohypnol is not approved for use in the United States, and its importation is banned
> Since about 1990, GHB (gamma hydroxybutyrate) has

been abused in the U.S. for its euphoric, sedative, and anabolic (body building) effects. It is a central nervous system depressant that was widely available over-the-counter in health food stores during the 1980s and until 1992. It was purchased largely by body builders to aid in fat reduction and muscle building. Street names include "liquid ecstasy," "soap," "easy lay," "vita-G," and "Georgia home boy." It renders the victim incapable of resisting, and may cause memory problems that could complicate case prosecution. In lower doses, GHB causes drowsiness, dizziness, nausea, and visual disturbances. At higher dosages, unconsciousness, seizures, severe respiratory depression, and coma can occur.

Combining abuse of GHB with other drugs such as alcohol can result in nausea and breathing difficulties. GHB may also produce withdrawal effects, including insomnia, anxiety, tremors, and sweating. GHB and two of its precursors, gamma butyrolactone (GBL) and 1,4 butanediol (BD), have been involved in poisonings, overdoses, date rapes, and deaths.

These drugs have also been used on men and women to facilitate committing other crimes, like robbery and physical assault. Alcohol, also, is often involved in date rape. Drinking alcohol can loosen inhibitions, dull common sense, and (for some people) allow aggressive tendencies to surface.

Most date rapes occur on college campuses. A national-level survey on 4,446 college women suggested that during any given academic year, 2.8 % of women will experience an attempted and/or completed rape. Most victims knew the person who sexually victimized them. For both completed and attempted rapes, about 9 in 10 offenders were known to the victim. Most often, a boyfriend, ex-boyfriend, classmate, friend, acquaintance, or coworker, sexually victimized the woman.[1]

The Temple of God

"Do you not know that you are the temple of God and that the Spirit of God dwells in you? If anyone defiles the temple of God, God will destroy him. For the temple of God is holy, which temple you are"
(1 Corinthians 3:16-17).

The Bible – in the Greek language – uses the word "naos" for the word "temple" in English. It is the inner portion of a Pharaonic or Greek temple. In it stood the statue of the deity to whom the temple was consecrated. It consists of the Holy place and the Holy of Holies. It is also used of the sanctuary where the image of gold was placed, which is *distinguished* from the whole enclosure. The word temple, in the verses mentioned above, also means the spiritual temple consisting of the saints of all ages, joined together by, and in, Christ.

You are, then, a dwelling place, a *distinguished* place, and a *sanctuary* where God Himself abides.

It is also written in the Gospel according to St. Luke (17:21) that "…the kingdom of God is within you."

We are the temple of God, and the kingdom of God is within us. God, the Holy, and *the* Holiness, is bestowing upon us this special grace and honor, to be His temple and sanctuary. Are we defiling it?

Always ask yourself: "Am I making my heart His dwelling abode?" "Am I corrupting and destroying God's temple?" God, our Father, the Holy One, wants us to live in holiness and purity.

♦ ♦ ♦ ♦ ♦ ♦ ♦

> "Oh, that they had such a heart in them
> that they would fear Me
> and always keep all My commandments,
> that it might be well with them
> and with their children forever!"
> (Deuteronomy 5:29).

Notes

1. The Sexual Victimization of College Women. Report from the U.S. Department of Justice, Office of Justice Programs, and National Institute of Justice released January 2001 regarding the sexual victimization of college women, on- and off-campus, including sexual assault, harassment, and stalking.

9

Studies and Statistics on Sexual Behaviors

Let us take a more detailed look at the problem of premarital sexual behaviors based on various statistics. The results and figures are disturbing.

(Note that it has been proven in several studies that having a boyfriend or girlfriend, especially an older one, leads to an increased initiation in adolescent sexual activity. The use of alcohol and drugs also initiates premarital sex early in life, and adds more problems to the original predicament. Also note that some people consider sex as vaginal intercourse only. They think that having other types of sexual behaviors are not necessarily "sex." They engage in such behaviors mainly out of fear of STDs and pregnancy. However, even with non-vaginal intercourse, individuals are prone to many diseases as well, and are still disobeying God).

1. Seventy-seven percent of 19-year-old females and 85% of 19-year-old males have engaged in sexual intercourse.[1]

2. The following data are from the 2002 National Survey of

Family Growth (NSFG), based on 12,571 – in-person interviews – with men and women 15-44 years of age.[2]

- At ages 15-19, about 12% of males and 10% of females have had heterosexual oral sex, but not vaginal intercourse. (Note that the male-female percentages are not significantly different). This percentage drops to 3% for both males and females at ages 22-24, when most have already had vaginal intercourse.

- Males 30-44 years of age reported an average (median) of 6-8 female sexual partners in their lifetimes. Among women 30-44 years of age, the median number of male sexual partners in their lifetimes was about four. The findings appear to be similar to previous surveys conducted in the early 1990's.

3. The Kaiser Family Foundation released the *National Survey of Adolescents and Young Adults: Sexual Health Knowledge, Attitudes, and Experiences, 2003*. The survey looks at a nationally representative sample of more than 1,800 people in three key age groups: young adolescents (ages 13-14), adolescents (ages 15-17), and young adults (ages 18-24). It asked these individuals about their knowledge and attitudes toward sexuality, as well as about their sexual experience – including sexual intercourse, oral sex, and intimacy.[3]

- 37% of adolescents, ages 15-17 (42% of males and 33% of females), reported having had sexual intercourse.

- 80% of adults, ages 18-24 (83% of males and 78% of females), reported having had sexual intercourse.

- Among adolescents ages 15-17 who had engaged in sexual intercourse, 11% reported having first had intercourse at 12 or 13, 44% at 14 or 15, and 37% at 16 or 17.

- Among adolescents, ages 15-17, who had engaged in sexual intercourse, 42% reported one lifetime partner, 39% reported 2-5 lifetime partners, 7% reported 6-9 lifetime partners, and 4% reported 10 or more lifetime partners.

- Among adults, ages 18-24, who had engaged in sexual intercourse, 20% reported one lifetime partner, 39% reported 2-5 lifetime partners, 13% reported 6-9 lifetime partners, and 14% reported 10 or more lifetime partners.

Regarding oral sex

- 36% of adolescents, ages 15-17, (40% of males and 32% of females), reported having had oral sex.

- 66% of young adults, ages 18-24, (73% of males and 58% of females), reported having had oral sex.

- 82% of adolescents and young adults, ages 15-24, who had engaged in sexual intercourse, reported having had oral sex.

- 24% of adolescents, ages 15-17 (18% of males and 33% of females), reported having had oral sex to avoid having intercourse.

Regarding intimacy

- 56% of adolescents, ages 15-17 (65% of males and 47% of females), reported having "been with someone in an intimate or sexual way (including but not limited to intercourse)."

- 85% of young adults ages, 18-24 (87% of males and 84% of females), reported having "been with someone in an intimate or sexual way (including but not limited to intercourse)."

4. Youth Risk Behavior Surveillance – United States, 2005.[4] It is believed that alcohol and drugs are mostly associated with sexual behaviors. This report summarizes results from the national survey, 40 state surveys, and 21 local surveys conducted among students in grades 9-12, during October 2004 to January 2006.

- Nationwide, 38.4% of students had used marijuana one or more times during their life.

- Nationwide, 25.6% of students drank alcohol (other than a few sips) for the first time before age 13 years.

- Nationwide, 14.3% of students had had sexual intercourse with ≥ 4 persons during their life.

- Among the 33.9% of currently sexually active students nationwide, 23.3% had alcohol and drugs associated with their sexual experience.

- By the 12th grade, 46.8% of teenagers have engaged in sexual intercourse.

5. "A study, which used statistics from the 1982, 1988, 1995 and 2002 National Survey of Family Growth, asked approximately 40,000 people, ages 15-44, about their sexual behavior. The study traced the trends in premarital sex back to the 1950's. Of those interviewed in 2002, 95% reported they had premarital sex; 93% said they did so by age 30. The study also showed that women born in the 1940s, nearly 90% had premarital sex. The 2005 data show that people are waiting longer to marry, and that the median age at first marriage was just over 25 for men and 27 for women."[5]

The above-mentioned data and statistics are significant, and reading them is quite alarming. It is time to wake up from living by the senses, which is taking us down in a whirlpool without our full awareness. That is one of the main reasons why going out on one-to-one basis should be reserved for a time when one is ready for marriage (and still without getting physically or sexually involved). Our Lord and Savior Jesus Christ wants us to live for Him, and by Him, to be safe, secure, holy and sanctified. Let us pray for the knowledge of the Truth that will set us free from all bondage of sin.

God's Intention

God's intention for sex was for procreation, for men and women to have a very special bond, and for enjoyment within the boundaries of marriage. Human beings altered God's purpose for sex to suit their own immoral desires.

It is a great misconception if we think that because sexual desire is natural, normal, and created by God, anything one does because of that desire is natural, and acceptable to God! Someone may then argue and say, "How can sexual desires, since they were created by God, be bad? He created everything and He said in Genesis that everything He created was good. Some scientists say that if you do not express those desires, you are suppressing them, and may eventually lead to perversion and many diseases." If Christians are accepting this way of thinking, they are disobeying God and dishonoring themselves. Sexual desire, if not tamed, will create a shallow, earthly, and lustful individual. On the other hand, living by the Spirit will create a balanced and mature personality.

> "I say then: Walk in the Spirit, and you shall not fulfill the lust of the flesh" (Galatians 5:16).

Unfortunately millions of people are living according to their basic instincts, especially when it comes to their sexual desires. These people are sinning against themselves as well as their partners and, above all, God, who is the Lover of mankind. We are not to degrade and devalue our human nature. Do not forget that we are God's children, and we were created in His own image (Genesis 1:27), and created to be His. God loves each one of us, and He is not happy watching His creation suffer from the consequences of sin. "For God so loved the world that He gave His only begotten Son, that whoever believes in Him should not perish but have everlasting life" (John 3:16). He created us to live a glorified life in this world, and not to run astray, and live a sinful life. He gave us free will. He offers us the choice: to love Him or leave Him, follow Him or follow our lusts.

Do We Have the Will?

Many have a strong conviction against premarital sex. Let's list some of the reasons for their belief.

- "It is a sin."
- "What am I missing out on – pregnancy, guilt, hurt, disease or abortion?"

- "AIDS is not curable. I want to avoid STDs."
- "Sex belongs only within the marriage boundaries."
- "To love someone is to wait."
- "Love is a commitment and not simply an act."
- "If a man loves a woman, he should love her as a person and not just as a body."
- "In obeying Him, there is full peace, joy and happiness."
- "We should be guided by our minds, and not by the desire of momentary pleasure."

A Way Out

If we are not deeply rooted in the word of God – if we do not have faith and trust in Him to lead our lives – we will certainly not be able to conquer our lusts and temptations. St. Paul said, "For those who live according to the flesh set their minds on the things of the flesh, but those *who live* according to the Spirit, the things of the Spirit" (Romans 8:5). He explained how those who are carnally minded choose to have their entire existence – body, soul and spirit – captivated by sin. He also said, "But the natural man does not receive the things of the Spirit of God, for they are foolishness to him; nor can he know *them*, because they are spiritually discerned" (1 Corinthians 2:14). The natural, or earthly, person considers spirituality as foolishness and even mocks the spiritual person.

Try to evaluate your life, and your relationships in the light of the word of God. If you find yourself lacking direction and strength, ask Him for help so that you can walk through life with purity and chastity. The more you value yourself as a child of the King of Kings, the more you will grow in your way toward Him and experience an inner peace. Philippians 4:7 reads, "and the peace of God, which surpasses all understanding, will guard your hearts and minds through

Christ Jesus." God, and only God, can grant you that inner peace and joy to live a holy life with a pure conscience.

For those who are still pure – keep yourselves in holiness and purity. For those who might have lost their purity – repent, ask for forgiveness without a moment's delay, and return to your heavenly Father with humility. His arms are open for everyone, irrespective of their past mistakes or their present situation. He will restore His tainted image, purify you, and create a new heart in you (Psalm 51). Be faithful, and avoid any further falls on the road. Let your life be in harmony with His word through prayer, confession, communion, and a daily encounter with the Lord.

Notes

1. The Urban Institute, "National Survey of Adolescent Males," National Institute of Child Health and Human Development, 1995. CDC "National Survey of Family Growth," 1995.

2. Sexual Behavior and Selected Health Measures: Men and Women 15-44 Years of Age, United States, 2002.
http://www.cdc.gov/nchs/products/pubs/pubd/ad/361-370/ad362.htm

3. National Survey of Adolescents and Young Adults: Sexual Health Knowledge, Attitudes, and Experiences" (#3218), The Henry J. Kaiser Family Foundation, May 2003. This information was reprinted with permission from the Henry J. Kaiser Family Foundation. The Kaiser Family Foundation, based in Menlo Park, California, is a nonprofit, private operating foundation focusing on the major health care issues facing the nation and is not associated with Kaiser Permanente or Kaiser Industries.

4. http://www.cdc.gov/mmwr/preview/mmwrhtml/SS5505a1.htm

5. Published in the January/ February 2007 issue of Public Health Reports, a peer-reviewed journal of the U.S. Public Health Service. Used with permission.

10

Called to Be Different

In a church meeting, the attendees were asked of their citizenship – to what country they belonged. Not surprisingly, they were puzzled. The question challenged them to think of their true citizenship, and to where they belonged. The speaker continued, "If you went to a foreign country for example, would people know from your accent that you were a foreigner? They certainly would. Moreover, if you went to any country in the whole world, you would be sort of an ambassador for your country. As a result, whatever you do, or say (either good or bad) will reflect on your place of citizenship."

The speaker sought to convey that we are only sojourners on this earth, and that our true citizenship is in heaven, and not in whatever country we were born. Our speech and behavior reflect our roots, what we ponder, and what our plans may be. So, if we think of heaven and the Lord of heavens everyday, our words and deeds will be inclined to be heavenly. If we do not think of heaven regularly, our thoughts, speech and actions will be worldly – in which case, we may need to revise our ways. St. Paul wrote,

> "For our citizenship is in heaven,
> from which we also eagerly wait for the Savior,
> the Lord Jesus Christ"
> (Philippians 3:20).

If our citizenship is in heaven, then we carry a heavenly passport, and do not belong to any one country. The blood of our Lord Jesus Christ grants us this citizenship. And everything we say, and do, should reflect our heavenly citizenship.

Our Good Savior, Jesus Christ, loves the whole world – saints and sinners, believers and non-believers. He wants everyone to know Him and live for Him. God "desires all men to be saved and to come to the knowledge of the truth" (1 Timothy 2:4).

Renew Your Mind

In the gospel according to St. John 17:14, the Lord Jesus Christ prayed and asked the Father, "I have given them Your word; and the world has <u>hated</u> them because they are <u>not of the world</u>, just as I am not of the world." Also in verse 16: "They are <u>not of the world</u>, just as I am not of the world." These are very strong statements, underlined by their repetition. How can we as Christians, being hated, live in the world although we are not of the world? The answer comes in verse 17: "Sanctify them by Your truth. Your word is truth." Being immersed and sanctified in the word of God (the truth), meditating and praying, are ways to live for Him on earth, and in the end we will reach our celestial city. Ephesians 4:17-18 states,

> "This I say, therefore, and testify in the Lord, that you should no longer walk as the rest of the Gentiles walk, in the

> <u>futility</u> of their mind, having their understanding darkened, being alienated from the life of God, because of the ignorance that is in them, because of the <u>blindness</u> of their heart."
>
> (In the American Standard Version, the word "futility" is replaced by "vanity." In the New American Standard Bible, the word "blindness" is replaced by "hardness").

These two verses actually are ground rules for living a Christian life. They involve the deeds: walk; thinking: mind, understanding, ignorance; heart: blind or hard. The end result is alienation from God. They are a maxim. St. Paul urged the Ephesians, as well as all of us, not to live like the rest of the world. These verses conclude that alienation from the life of God, results in our estrangement and separation from Him.

You may ask, "As a Christian, what do I learn from these two verses?" The core issue here is living on earth in a manner that pleases the Lord. Ask yourself in every situation and occasion: "Will the Lord Jesus, the Holy One, accept this thought, action or behavior? Will He accept to be in the place where I am, and agreeable to the conversations that I have? If I were to judge my life against the Holy Scriptures, will I be found wanting – (Daniel 5:27)."

Be honest and faithful with your answers. Whether we live in light or in darkness, our thoughts and deeds will reflect our way of living.

Verse 19 of the same chapter continues, "who, being <u>past feeling</u>, have given themselves over to <u>lewdness</u>, to work all <u>uncleanness</u> with greediness." The NASB translation reads, "and they, having become <u>callous</u>, have given themselves over to <u>sensuality</u> for the practice of every kind of <u>impurity</u> with greediness."

Those people, having lost all sensitivity (their hearts were stony hard – callous), had given themselves over to sensuality so as to indulge in every kind of impurity, with a continual and unquenchable lust, not wanting to hear anything that condemned their behavior.

Verses 22-24 read, "that you put off, concerning your former conduct, the old man which grows corrupt according to the deceitful lusts, and be renewed in the spirit of your mind, and that you put on the new man which was created according to God, in true righteousness and holiness." So, as Christians, we are different in the way we manage our lives. We need to put off the old conduct (that belongs to the world, and which grows corrupt according to the deceitful lusts), and be renewed in the spirit of our mind. Finally, we put on the new man, which was created according to God, in true righteousness and holiness.

Also in Colossians 3:3-11, St. Paul advised us to put to death our earthly desires and actions, and put on the new man which is renewed in knowledge according to the image of Him who created him. By putting to death the earthly, old man, and putting on the spiritual, new man, we will continually grow in the knowledge and understanding of our Lord and Savior Jesus Christ. Romans 12:2 says,

> "And do not be conformed to this world,
> but be transformed by the renewing of your mind,
> that you may prove what *is* that good and
> acceptable and perfect will of God."

In Merriam-Webster's online dictionary, 10th edition, the definition of "conform" is:
  a) To be similar or identical; to be in agreement or harmony.
  b) To be obedient or compliant; to act in accordance with prevailing standards or customs.

The definition of "transform" (same dictionary) is:
a) To change in composition or structure.
b) To change the outward form or appearance.
c) To change in character or condition: convert.

St. Paul advised us not to be one and the same with the world around us, but to change our composition, or structure (transform). This change is not only in our heart's desires, but also in our intentions, thoughts, inner attributes, and actions.

How can we accomplish that transformation? It is accomplished by constantly renewing our minds. And how can we renew our minds? The mind is renewed through repentance, being exposed to the word of God daily, and allowing the Holy Spirit to work in our lives.

My Life in Christ

On another occasion, St. Paul also said, "For to me, to live *is* Christ, and to die *is* gain" (Philippians 1:21). To have a life is to have it from the Lord Jesus Christ Himself, and behave and act as it were His life. Second Corinthians 5:15 reads, "and He died for all, that those who live should live no longer for themselves, but for Him who died for them and rose again." The life that I live is not my life, but His. I am the one who was supposed to die for my sins; instead, He died for me on the cross, and gave me His life. I am now alive in Him. Galatians 2:20 reads, "I have been crucified with Christ; it is no longer I who live, but Christ lives in me; and the *life* which I now live in the flesh I live by faith in the Son of God, who loved me and gave Himself for me."

We are to enjoy our lives to the maximum, in holiness and godliness. The world is not bad or awful, but the corruption, due to sin, made living with (and for) the Lord to be a struggle. In living as He lived, we will be able to overcome, and avoid, the immoral and indecent conduct that the world teaches us. We are exposed, on a daily basis, with many unhealthy and immoral worldly venues that may fill our hearts, minds and souls. We need to be spiritually well equipped to be able to live in the world, as we are not of the world. Our relationships with others will be pure, sanctified, and holy. Understanding and having a full conviction that we belong to heaven, and not the world, will support and protect us from falling into the many traps Satan prepares for us.

Real Life Examples

Kathy, 19, was sharing her dorm room with a non-Christian girl. She mentioned that a life of purity, and chastity, became increasingly difficult for her. Living in a college dorm, with all its distractions, made it very difficult for Kathy to live as a true Christian. She could not read the Bible, nor have her own quiet time with the Lord as regularly as she used to. She tried to associate herself with godly people in the dorm, yet she still had a difficult time overcoming all the temptations. Kathy needed to find the Way in the midst of all the distractions. That by itself was a challenge for her.

An illustration of this situation (being discouraged by the conduct of other people) is in 2 Peter 2:7-8, "and delivered righteous Lot, *who was* oppressed by the filthy conduct of the wicked, (for that righteous man, dwelling among them, tormented *his* righteous soul from day to day by seeing and hearing *their* lawless deeds)."

In a way, Lot's story was similar to what was happening to Kathy. Kathy tried to dissociate herself somewhat from dorm life by finding a place where she could have her quiet time and pray. She recalled that her priest, at her church back home, had told her of a church nearby her school.

She finally found the church, and started attending there regularly.

Another example is the story of Chris, 20, who expressed his desire to live a life of purity and chastity. Because of this longing, he had hoped not to dorm at college, thereby avoiding all the temptations and distractions of dorm life. However, the attractions and the excitement, associated with dorm life, were too strong for him. Although his home was only twenty minutes from the college, he opted to stay at the dorm.

Little by little, Chris started conforming to the world around him, instead of being transformed, as the Bible describes. He soon started dropping classes, and changed his major to an easier one, so he could have more time for "fun." His mind was occupied with his extra-curricular activities. Consequently, he was unable to study regularly and his grades were well below average.

Another example: Josh, 22, who was living in the dorm. When some church members visited him in the evening, he indicated that he was done with his studies for the day. They asked him what he was planning to do for the rest of the evening. "Nothing," he replied nonchalantly. They were astonished that the entire evening was to be wasted on "nothing." Then they informed him that there was another man who lived next door, who actually used to attend his church. They offered that they could get together to pray, read the Bible, or even start a small Bible study class. He replied, "I had never thought of that." They tried to encourage Josh, as the Lord had encouraged them, to grow more and more in the spiritual life.

Being in the dorm, and at that time of the day, his colleagues were mostly hanging out with each other, or partying. He was living as others did, either intentionally or unintentionally (Birds of a feather flock together).

It's true that we need to spend time with our friends. We also need to be cognizant of the amount of time that we spend with them. Moderation is beneficial. In addition, without our awareness, we may imitate many of our friends' characters and behaviors. Josh needed a reminder that everything he was thinking of, or doing, should have been for the glory of our Lord and Savior Jesus Christ. Be mindful that we have a higher calling – to be the Lord's.

Ruth, 26, was from a strong Christian family. She went to church regularly, and helped in several activities. Her father passed away two years ago. She was supporting her ailing mother and her younger sister. In the morning, she went to school, attended classes, and studied in the library. In the evening, she worked as a waitress in a restaurant. At work, she was approached by several men to go out with, or just have "fun" for sometime. She declined going out with anyone of them, seeing that they were not serious. At several occasions, she was tempted to go out with a few of them, but her dedication and commitment to the Lord were stronger. The word of God was in her heart, and on her mouth. Being from a Christian family, and truly practicing her Christian life, made her a strong person in front of temptations. Her true delight was in the Lord and His commandments, as the Psalmist says, "Blessed *is* the man Who walks not in the counsel of the ungodly, Nor stands in the path of sinners, Nor sits in the seat of the scornful; But his delight *is* in the law of the LORD, And in His law he meditates day and night" (Psalm 1:1-2). For her, a serious commitment in a relationship was crucial. She did not want to live by what the world may dictate, but the law of the Lord was her life. She had a lot on her plate, and she did not want to spend time with any of those men. Her plan was to go out with the individual who was serious, and truly committed for a relationship in the Lord. In addition, she wanted to wait until she finished her studies. At this phase of her life, her obligations at home were also vital.

> "...having escaped the corruption *that is* in the world through lust" (2 Peter 1:4).

As Christians, we are called to be different; and important key factors in our life are our commitment, and inner conviction to be different. We need to use our time in the best possible way, not neglecting any one aspect of our lives. We also should set priorities and re-evaluate them constantly to check whether we are still on the right track or not.

Light and Salt

These true accounts underscore the fact that our surroundings, and our inner convictions, play important roles in influencing our conduct and behavior. We are also reminded that our citizenship is not an issue to be forgotten or ignored, but a major lifelong commitment to our heavenly Father.

> "For we are His workmanship,
> created in Christ Jesus for good works,
> which God prepared beforehand
> that we should walk in them"
> (Ephesians 2:10).

Our Lord Jesus Christ knows what is good for us, and He prepared a whole plan and a path for us (Jeremiah 29:11). The main point is to know them, and walk in them faithfully.

We are also to remind ourselves that our Lord and Savior Jesus Christ is the Light. It is through our citizenship and union with Him, that we are the light and salt of the earth (Matthew 5:13-14). It is then, natural, that we will shine, and make life tasteful to those around us. Our Lord Jesus Christ did not say, "You *should be* the light and salt," or,

"*Try your best* to be what I am telling you," but He said plainly that we *are* the light and salt of the earth!

11

Ways to Be Different

In this chapter we will discuss how we can live by the Biblical guidelines that were described in the previous chapter, as citizens of heaven on earth. The following is a list of topics that may serve as a guide to living "differently:"

- Live in a spiritual and healthy environment.
- Read His words and spiritual books.
- Participate in Church Sacraments.
- Attend spiritual meetings.
- Pray.
- Seek guidance.
- Start serving and be active.
- Try to excel in your career.
- Use your time effectively.

1. <u>Live in a spiritual and healthy environment.</u>

The influence of the environment on an individual is greatly underestimated. If we surround ourselves with godly people, then we will tend to become godly as well. The opposite is also true, if we surround ourselves with people living in a worldly manner. Could the good apples in a basket stay unblemished, if there is only one rotten apple in the bunch?

If you go out with a group that talks about sex and sexuality, will you be able to refrain from joining in on the jesting, and to resist the possibility of being drawn toward sexually explicit speech and behavior. If the group you are spending time with does not promote healthy habits and interests, you may start drifting away from the right path.

You need to evaluate your relationships. You may find that it would be to your best interest to minimize the time you spend with those who harm your thinking and spirit. Start acquainting yourself with a church group that is pursuing a righteous path and interested in growing spiritually. Just as unhealthy habits and temptations are contagious; so are purity, holiness, and sanctity. We read in 1 Corinthians 15:33-34, "Do not be deceived: 'Evil company corrupts good habits.' Awake to righteousness and do not sin; for some do not have the knowledge of God. I speak *this* to your shame.'"

We should be aware not only of the people around us, but also of any other influence in our environment. Certain music, internet sites, and places we go to, can stimulate unspiritual and demoralizing ideas and desires. These influences contradict the purity of a Christian lifestyle. Rather than bringing us down, we should try to ensure that our environment is helping us live a godly life.

2. Read His words and spiritual books.

In John 6:63, the Lord Jesus Christ said, "It is the Spirit who gives life; the flesh profits nothing. The words that I speak to you are spirit, and *they* are life." The following story is from the early Christian desert Fathers, and illustrates how the words of God are vital to our lives:

There was a spiritual father who lived in the desert during the early Christian centuries. He had a disciple who used to go to him for guidance in reading and understanding the Bible. The father told his disciple to go to his own room, pray and read. After a while the disciple came back, and the father asked him what he understood. The disciple replied that he didn't understand much. The father told him once more to go, pray and read. After a while the disciple again returned and the spiritual father who once again asked him, "My son, did you understand anything?" The disciple answered, "a little." Surprisingly, the father again gave the same advice, which was to go, pray and read. A few days later, the disciple returned and the spiritual father asked the same question, "Did you understand anything?" The disciple answered, "A little more."

At this point, the father asked the disciple to bring a basket made of palm leaves and to fill it with water. Since obedience is essential in monastic discipleship, he obeyed – knowing that the basket will not be filled, since it was made of leaves and twigs. He did so several times and the water kept seeping out. He returned to the father saying that it was impossible because of the holes in the basket. The father then asked him, "What happened every time you filled the basket with water?" The disciple answered, "The water leaked out." The father then asked, "What happened to the basket each time you filled it up?" The disciple said, "Well, it got cleaner." So the father finally said, "Just like the effect of the water on the basket, the words of God can cleanse us from all impurities. Even if our minds could not contain them – not reaching understanding – still, they purify our souls."

Get yourself in the habit of reading the Bible every single day. To read one chapter in the Bible takes only a few minutes. A compact Bible can easily be placed in your purse or briefcase. Read during your ten-minute breaks, or whenever you are free. There are many opportunities, just plan for these breaks, and take the time to read.

When Veronica used to ride the subways in New York, she saw Jews reading the Torah, Christians reading the Bible, and Muslims reading the Koran. So she said to herself, "If they could manage to read, I also could read." She then started the habit of reading in transit.

In addition to the Bible, read spiritual books. Read about the saints and how they lived a holy and sanctified life. Read about the spiritual life, heaven, and all the angelic hosts. Search your local church bookstore or the many internet web sites. You will find hundreds, if not thousands, of references on spiritual topics. Do not give yourself the excuse that you are not a reader, or that it's boring.

One time a church member gave a Bible to a woman and encouraged her to read it daily. However, she told him that she was not in the habit of reading. A few weeks later, he saw her again. She told him that while on vacation with her two daughters, she had read an entire book on the plane. A week after her return, while cleaning her house, she found the Bible he had given her. She said to herself, "If I finished a whole book in that short period of time on the plane, I could indeed read the entire Bible." She began to do so from that point on.

There is a quotation that says: "There is a great hope for every sinner who reads the Bible; and there is the greatest danger for the greatest saint who does not read the Bible."

"Your words were found, and I ate them, And Your word was to me the joy and rejoicing of my heart; For I am called by Your name, O LORD God of hosts"
(Jeremiah 15:16).

"Take the trouble to read the books, for they will save you from impurity"
(St. Anthony the Great – 3rd - 4th century A.D.).

"Be diligent in reading the lives of the saints so that you are inflamed with envy of their works"
(St. Anthony the Great).

"The mind can not approach God without reading the divine Book" (St. Isaac the Syrian – 7th century A.D.).

"Have a boundless love for the reading of the Psalms for they are spiritual food" (St. Isaac the Syrian).

3. **Participate in Church Sacraments.**

Participating in the Church Sacraments, and attending the various services and liturgies (on a regular basis and with a pure intention), are protective practices to help us live for the Lord.

The Lord said, "He who eats My flesh and drinks My blood abides in Me, and I in him" (John 6:56). Abiding in the Lord, and the Lord in you, is one of the greatest gifts our Lord gave us. Can you imagine an enemy harming you, while you are in the protection of the Strongest Castle – the Lord Himself?

Through our continuous cleansing by means of repentance, confession and communion, we grow spiritually and live a holy and sanctified life pleasing the Lord. On the other hand, by not participating in the sacraments, we actually leave our weapons, let down our guards, and get exposed to the darts of Satan, and who can stand them alone? We need to empower ourselves by abiding in the Almighty through the Church Sacraments and prayers.

4. <u>Attend spiritual meetings.</u>

Spiritual meetings provide the basic instructions for salvation. We will also be protected from wrong ideas and accusations against our Christian faith, which others may try to instill in our minds. Spiritual meetings help us live with a strong spiritual stance.

You may not benefit one hundred percent from each meeting, but it all adds up over time. Keep your senses open to spiritualities until they become your way of life. Do not be discouraged if you find people in those meetings that seem to be more spiritual than you are. Also, do not be discouraged by those who turn out not to be as spiritual as you had thought. Soon you will find out with whom you should acquaint yourself. Meetings and conferences are not for saints, but for everyone, and every level of spirituality. Regardless, you will definitely benefit from the Bible studies, the songs, and the fellowship itself, which will help you grow spiritually.

5. <u>Pray.</u>

We need to experience prayer and its power. The more you pray and get closer to the Lord, the more you will know Him and love Him. Pray with the Psalms or the Book of the Hours; they will help you throughout your journey on earth. Prayer is one of the best practices for our spiritual growth. Stay connected with heaven daily. Prayer gets more tasteful over time. Keep this hotline to heaven always open. It's free, and you never need customer service. You start talking, and you are right there, connected – without interruption. No one will cut you off, nor will you receive a busy signal. Unfortunately, we are the ones who will interrupt the connection, or get busy with other things.

St. Arsenius, one of the early Christian desert Fathers (4th – 5th century A.D.), used to pray continuously from sunset to sunrise. However, this does not necessarily mean that everyone will do the same. He was a monk living in the desert, while we are busy with work, families, and many other obligations. On the other hand, do not tell yourself that you are not a saint, and neglect in your prayers.

Start this very personal relationship with Him today. Talk to Him as a friend with all your needs, problems, and love toward Him. Our Lord is happy listening to us pray, even if it's only for a few minutes. If you do not know how to pray, try thinking of someone who is in need of help, and ask God earnestly, to help this person. You will discover the joy, peace and humility that you will gain by praying for others.

Your prayers will grow with you as you grow spiritually. Read the story of Abraham talking with God in Genesis 18, and see how he was interceding for Sodom and Gomorrah. Just as Abraham had this conversation with God, we too can speak with Him in the same way. Yet, do not forget that we are interacting with the Creator of the Universe. What an honor He has granted us to freely talk with Him!

"Prayer is the raising of the mind to God" (St. John of Damascus – 7th-8th century A.D.).

"Prayer is a great weapon, an enduring treasure and unfading riches" (St. John Chrysostom).

"It is impossible for the soul to possess any virtue without prayer" (St. John Chrysostom).

"He who neglects prayer and thinks that there is another door to repentance, is deceived by the devil" (St. Isaac the Syrian).

6. Seek guidance.

One of the saints said, "Those who are without guidance are like the leaves of the trees; they easily fall." Choose your guidance from those people who have an ear ready to listen, a compassionate heart, a lot of experience, and a sound mind in the Lord. Your friend, or colleague, may be ready to hear about your situation, but may not have sufficient experience and spiritual maturity to be able to advise you properly. There are bishops, priests, church leaders, deacons, servants, and holy people whom you can trust, and who can guide you.

7. Start serving.

Serving others requires effort, time, and above all, love. However, in serving others, you will be delighted to help out and meet the needs of others. Yet, service is not completely all about giving. We gain many attributes from our experiences and most importantly, service is living as our Master lived. He came to serve and not to be served. "For even the Son of Man did not come to be served, but to serve, and to give His life a ransom for many" (Mark 10:45).

God wanted to use Moses the prophet to serve His people. Moses was hesitant and came up with several excuses. But God commanded him and he became the spokesman of God. Similarly, in one church, many women and men were asked to serve. They were very hesitant and claimed that they did not possess the necessary qualifications for service. However, the life of service is not just about our level or degree of qualifications, but our willingness and faithfulness to try to emulate our Lord Jesus Christ.

Start attending classes to be a Sunday school teacher, while adding more to your experience from Bible reading, spiritual books, and meetings. When you eventually do serve, you will find real joy and peace. Ask your church leaders about the different services that are available that may suit your life and time, and not necessarily Sunday school. If you are already a teacher, then participate more fervently. Pray for the people you are serving. Be attentive to their needs, and be close to them in happiness and in sorrow. In addition, try to serve the elderly and those who do not have anyone to serve them.

8. Excel in your career.

As Christians, we are to strive to excel in our careers. It will please the Lord that we are earnestly attempting to succeed. Apply for a masters or a doctorate degree. Search how you can grow in your field of experience. In your search for excellence, do not forget to help out your brothers and sisters who may be in the early steps of their career paths.

9. Use your time effectively.

Use your time in a way that will build you up. For example, people who play sports or work out regularly, usually say that they feel rejuvenated after exercising. They feel more energetic; they're in shape; and they're healthier. Having a healthy body is beneficial for you. Christianity does not degrade or debase the body; on the contrary, it respects it. The body needs to be under the control of the spirit, and ultimately, the Holy Spirit.

There are also many hobbies that could enrich your character, like camping, fishing, hiking, etc. By having a healthy body, and abstaining from destructive activities, one will be less prone, by the grace of God, to succumb to the darts and temptations of the devil.

Finally, our spirits need to be united with the Spirit of God. Our souls need to be satisfied through good and edifying activities. "A satisfied soul loathes the honeycomb, But to a hungry soul every bitter thing *is* sweet" (Proverbs 27:7). If we are satiated with the Lord and His sweetness, then we will not so readily run to the various distractions that we may come across.

A Prayer

Lord, we pray that every man and every woman may know You and know how sweet You are.

Let each one, Lord, be strong in front of the powerful temptations they face everyday.

Let them witness to You through their faithfulness, sincerity and purity.

Guard them and save them from the tempest of the sea of this world.

Give them wisdom and understanding to flee from sin, and run to Your loving arms.

Lift them up through Your Holy Spirit, and let them grasp a glimpse of the heavenly.

Show them, Lord, that life on earth is nothing but a shadow, and that eternity is what we should long for.

Keep them always in Your heart.

And Lord, as the Lover of mankind, if we sin; willingly or unwillingly; knowingly or unknowingly, please forgive and remit all our iniquities, and renew the work of Your Holy Spirit in us.

12

Living in Purity

Many people do not have a clear perception of what purity represents. Some may mistakenly believe that to be pure, or chaste, one must simply refrain from having sexual relations. Others believe that purity is attained by overcoming certain specific sins; like lying, cheating, cursing, anger, etc.

The definition of *pure* (Merriam-Webster's online dictionary, 10th edition) is:
 a) Free from dust, dirt, or taint
 b) Spotless
 c) Free from moral fault or guilt
 d) Marked by chastity

Whereas the definition of *chastity* (same dictionary) is:
 a) Abstention from unlawful sexual intercourse
 b) Purity in conduct and intention

Pure also means "natural" – as originally intended and created by God. It is like a seed planted in soil void of any impurities. Just as God planned for the seed to be "natural," and grow in a pure environment, so also God intended for us to grow in a pure and untainted environment.

Purity Tainted

But can our lives become impure? They may, if our lives are not continually cleansed by repentance. In addition, the devil also does his best (or worst) to distract us from the life of purity. "So the great dragon was cast out, that serpent of old, called the Devil and <u>Satan, who deceives the whole world</u>; he was cast to the earth, and his angels were cast out with him" (Revelation 12:9). Also, St Paul mentioned, "lest Satan should take advantage of us; for we are not ignorant of his devices" (2 Corinthians 2:11). Satan constantly deceives people to fall into sinful and impure thoughts, actions and deeds.

Sin is a force that pulls us down, while purity lifts us up. Sin is depression, while purity is everlasting joy.

St. Paul urged us not to use our bodies to commit sins, or to lead others to sin; but to use them for the glory of God. "And do not present your members *as* instruments of unrighteousness to sin, but present yourselves to God as being alive from the dead, and your members *as* instruments of righteousness to God" (Romans 6:13). Each part of our human body should be consecrated to serve the Lord and to spread His Kingdom. Your feet will lead you to places of worship and fellowship, your tongue will speak about Him, your eyes will see His hands working mightily, and your heart will long for His love.

Despite our possible straying and the devil's influence, we can control our "impure" tendencies through the work of the Holy Spirit in us, our daily spiritual satiety with the Lord, and by putting on the full armor of God (Ephesians 6).

> "All the ways of a man *are* pure in his own eyes, But the LORD weighs the spirits" (Proverbs 16:2).

Strive with Perseverance

The life of purity is a virtue that is attainable through an inward struggle, vigilance, and above all, the grace of God. Purity is a continuous practice in which we need to control our whole being, and sanctify it for God. Our bodies, instincts and spirits need to be controlled; otherwise they will control us. They may lead us down a path not intended by God. By living a true life of prayer, fasting, spiritual exercises, practicing the sacraments, and attending church regularly, we will be able to grow in the life of purity. (Note that at times we may be fooling ourselves into thinking we are living pure lives, but without a genuine inner conviction, holiness, or sanctity. What is being practiced is merely a façade, while the inner life might be decaying. In essence, we would be living a great deception).

God is pure, His words are pure, and He is asking us to be pure as He is. Habakkuk 1:13 says, "*You are* of purer eyes than to behold evil, And cannot look on wickedness..." Psalm 12:6 says, "The words of the LORD *are* pure words, *Like* silver tried in a furnace of earth, Purified seven times."

If we really want to see the Lord, purity is the way, and the condition. Our Lord Jesus Christ said in Matthew 5:8, "Blessed *are* the pure in heart, For they shall see God." Purity is one of the cornerstones of the Christian spiritual life, and its victory. It is the garment of the saints that they longed for; and for its sake they denied all earthly pleasures.

In trying to live in purity, one needs to fight to avoid evil, and all its forms. "Flee sexual immorality. Every sin that a man does is outside the body, but he who commits sexual immorality sins against his own body. Or do you not know that your body is the temple of the Holy Spirit *who is* in you, whom you have from God, and you are not your own? For you were bought at a price; therefore, glorify God in your body and in your spirit, which are God's"

(1 Corinthians 6:18-20). Also, 1 Thessalonians 5:21-22 reads, "Test all things; hold fast what is good. Abstain from every form of evil." What did the Bible mean by "every form of evil?" There are certain evils that are disguised – appearing as harmless lambs; but in reality, they are ravaging wolves. There are many thoughts and ideas than can cross our mind, but are they all pure? A thought may seem simple and innocent, but in fact it may hide a string of other thoughts that may be inappropriate, unclear, corrupt, and may lead to immoral actions. Do not let thoughts dwell and grow in your mind before you present them to the Lord, and His light. He will then guide you to the right and appropriate one. You have to "Keep your heart with all diligence, For out of it *spring* the issues of life" (Proverbs 4:23).

"Beloved, now we are children of God; and it has not yet been revealed what we shall be, but we know that when He is revealed, we shall be like Him, for we shall see Him as He is. And everyone who has this hope in Him purifies himself, just as He is pure" (1 John 3:2-3).

Is it Unrealistic?

No one should think that the path to purity is impossible. Do not be discouraged. With God's help, it is far from difficult. God's word in the Bible inspires us and gives us spirit and life (John 6:63). The Lord Jesus asked of God the Father, "Sanctify them by Your truth. Your word is truth" (John 17:17). God will sanctify our lives through living in His truth. Being sanctified by the Lord (and *for* the Lord), we will be able to live in purity and enjoy life with Him. We will then grow from one level of purity to the next, by the grace of God.

"The law of the LORD *is* perfect, converting the **soul**; The testimony of the LORD *is* sure, making **wise** the simple;

The statutes of the LORD *are* <u>right,</u> rejoicing the **heart**; The commandment of the LORD *is* <u>pure</u>, enlightening the **eyes**; The fear of the LORD *is* clean, enduring forever; The judgments of the LORD *are* <u>true</u> *and* <u>righteous</u> altogether. More to be desired *are they* than gold, Yea, than much fine gold; Sweeter also than honey and the honeycomb. Moreover by them Your servant is warned, *And* in keeping them *there is* great reward" (Psalm 19:7-11).

(His words are perfect, sure, right, pure, true and righteous).

It is amazing how the word of God can encompass all aspects of our lives. The soul, the mind, the heart, and the eyes – if they are in the realm of the word of God – they will be transformed, made wise, and enlightened.

The Story of Mike

Mike, 25, had just graduated from college and was very excited about starting a new phase of his life. He soon obtained his first job at a large financial firm. His friends were very happy for him, and felt that this would be a great time for him to find a significant other. They pushed Mike to find a "girlfriend," like some of them had. Their opinions were based merely on having fun, and not necessarily on the potential of a serious relationship, and possibly marriage.

They drew his attention to Liz, 24, one of his previous classmates who had liked him. Nonetheless, he was adamant about not getting involved with anyone just for the fun of it. He firmly expressed his opinions, and went on to say that if he were interested in someone, it would be with the intention of pursuing a serious relationship – one which could potentially lead to marriage.

Mike also had many things to accomplish before sharing his heart and life with his future spouse – mainly, to deepen his relationship with the Lord, gain more experience in life, and explore his career potential. For Mike, this growth was necessary in order to enable him to take on the huge responsibility of being a husband and a father. He did want to get married eventually, but needed to prepare himself for that phase of his life. He also added that since he was not yet ready for a commitment, he did not want to waste someone's time, or play with their emotions.

Which is wiser: To swim in turbulent waters and foggy surroundings or to wait until the waves are calm and visibility improves? For Mike, stability and direction were two essential keystones in his life. He insisted that the waves would only toss him around, causing him to grow tired, and possibly drown. Being determined to belong to the Lord, and not to the world, was an important factor in the strength of Mike's stand. He had faith that, when the time for marriage is right, it will be crystal clear. He was striving to live a life of purity and chastity. He was taking Joseph, from the Old Testament, as his role model.

He referred to Biblical examples, like those of Joseph, David, and Tamar, which illustrate how sin can be (1) consuming (in the story of Potiphar's wife with Joseph, Genesis 39); (2) appealing, yet deceiving (in the story of David, 2 Samuel 11); and (3) ruining (in the story of Amnon with Tamar, 2 Samuel 13).

God sent His Holy Spirit so that we live a pure, chaste, and sanctified life. It is vital to be pure in mind, soul, spirit and heart – unyielding to the schemes of the devil, not giving him the chance to pollute our lives. God is delighted when He sees His children strong in times of temptation, and even more pleased when they avoid the temptation altogether.

As for Mike, rejecting his friends' suggestion to pursue Liz was not easy for him because he used to think of her. At one point, he thought of her as a potential spouse. He had resisted his initial attraction toward her, for he knew that the Lord is gracious, and did not want to pursue the relationship based on worldly standards. He knew that if God wanted them to be together, He would eventually bring them together at the right time.

Mike was in a difficult situation with his friends. He might have been perceived as being arrogant, or labeled as odd, strange, and at sometimes even mocked. The more they argued, the more he found reason to hold his ground. As time went on, they were getting frustrated with him. Although he actually loved them with all his heart, he was more concerned with pleasing the Lord, rather than his friends. "Since you have purified your souls in obeying the truth through the Spirit in sincere love of the brethren, love one another fervently with a pure heart" (1 Peter 1:22).

Changes Happen

You could see the power and strength in Mike's life, in that he was able to set a powerful example. He advised his friends to be careful in their own dealings with women, not to try to attract them by sweet-talking them (since a charmer can easily grasp a woman's attention and heart). They should be more sincere, and honest in their conversations. They should also avoid saying or acting in a way to express any affection, or flirting with women. Simply talking to women in suggestive ways can lead them to develop illusions, hopes, and inappropriate thoughts. Likewise, some women may mislead men. However, no one should play with another's heart.

One of Mike's friends became convinced of his ways, and decided to wait until he was spiritually mature before pursuing a relationship. Another friend ended a relationship with his girlfriend that was more of a romance and a lust. Subsequently, the three of them became more involved in church. Together, they started a prayer meeting, and prayed that the rest of their friends would also join them. That prayer meeting is still growing and, at the time of writing this book, fifteen people were attending it regularly. The meeting created spiritual bonds and fellowship, and became an encouragement to many.

Another very essential milestone in Mike's story is the continuous assessment of the purity of his heart. As time goes on, our conviction may weaken, due to various reasons. Therefore, a constant evaluation, and replenishing the heart with the word of God, is of major importance.

The story of Mike is like a breath of fresh air to many men and women. Surely, any woman who truly loves the Lord will respect Mike dearly, when she notes his behavior and ideals. Many women would want to marry a man such as Mike, rather than those who seek momentary pleasures, or who carelessly jump from one relationship to the next.

Footsteps to Follow

Mike's story could be your story, or the story of someone you know. We need to follow the examples of those who live such a pure lifestyle. Song of Solomon 1:8 reads, "If you do not know, O fairest among women, follow in the footsteps of the flock, and feed your little goats beside the shepherds' tents." Here, the "flock" refers to those saints and holy people who longed, from all their hearts, to be the Lord's, and lived the life of purity and holiness.

Start praying to the Lord. Ask Him from all your heart, mind, and soul to cleanse you from all impurities, and to show you the right path. Repent, confess, and start a new phase in your life. The more you are purified and refined, the more you will love to dedicate yourself to the Lord. He will lead you, step by step, through this beautiful life where you can see Him, enjoy His Fatherhood, and live for Him.

♦ ♦ ♦ ♦ ♦ ♦ ♦

13

Steps to Engagement

> "Who can find a virtuous wife? For her
> worth *is* far above rubies"
> (Proverbs 31:10).

Alfred, 28, was working as a business consultant in Toronto, while finishing his masters. A year ago, he thought of Deborah, a 25-year-old pharmacist, as a potential spouse. He had to wait to be more settled in his career, as well as in other aspects of his life before pursuing a relationship. Both Deborah and Alfred had been attending the same church for several years. They were involved in quite a few activities where he observed her eagerness to help people. She was pleasant, very active in the Bible study class; and always had creative ideas that she strived to implement. He knew her family that was well respected in the congregation.

Deborah started helping in the children's summer camp, in which Alfred was also volunteering. He observed how she treated the children, even when they were so rambunctious. She expressed her true love and respect for them, without being repulsed. He valued her patience and compassion. So far, she seemed to be the kind of person with whom he would like to share his life. However, Alfred noted a couple of attributes that raised questions in his mind.

He noticed that she was spending a lot of money on the kids. He did not mind giving them gifts and toys, but his opinion was that her gifts were a bit excessive. He was not sure if Deborah's way of spending money on the kids was because she liked them so much, or because it was her style of living. He wondered, "When she gets married, will she be spending uncontrollably?" It was a point that needed further observation and clarification.

Another point he pondered was the fact that she spent too much time in church. He thought, "Will she share responsibilities at home, or ignore them?"

He prayed and consulted with his spiritual father, his parents, and some of his friends. Despite his concerns, he finally decided to express his interest to her. He thought either of two outcomes would result. The first outcome is that she would decline his interest, which would disappoint him for a time. The second outcome is that she would share his interest in pursuing a relationship and exploring the potential of a future together. At any rate, he wanted the will of the Lord to be done.

In due time

Months later, Alfred took advantage of an opportunity at a church picnic and expressed his feelings of admiration to Deborah. He realized that she did not have any special feelings for him. For her, Alfred was an average looking individual, but had good qualities. She responded by asking him for time to pray about it in the upcoming weeks. She needed this time to pray, think and ask others for advice.

She spoke with her priest and one of the spiritual leaders in the church who knew Alfred well. Both recommended Alfred and offered to pray for them to see what God may reveal. In the mean time, they told her that she needed to get to know him personally, since the final decision is hers and not anyone else's. She appreciated Alfred's honesty and sincerity, as well as other qualities he had; but she was not sure if he was the right person.

Finally, she chose to focus on those valuable qualities of his, as opposed to the superficial ones. She thought that what will last is not the appearance or looks, but the attributes that the person will bring to the relationship. She told him that she would like to get to know him better. She also informed her family about him and about her decision. They were happy and supportive, and promised to pray for both of them. Few weeks later, Alfred visited her family. They were very pleased with his personality and demeanor.

Going out

They started going out, and discussed many issues, concerns, and got to know each other. In time, Deborah felt more and more comfortable with Alfred. Her priest also talked with them several times. He was happy about how they were conducting themselves, and he continued to pray for both of them. He advised them not to be influenced by the waves of romance that may fluctuate easily, and to continue praying that the Lord may guide them and show them His will. They agreed, and said that they had thought of those same things, and added that they wanted to keep their minds pure.

Concerns

Alfred did not want either one of them to simply impress the other, while hiding negative attributes that would be unaccepted to the other individual. He wanted the reality without modifications or sugarcoating.

Alfred discussed with her, frankly and openly, his concerns regarding spending money, and all the time she spends in church. She was honest and told him that she could not resist spending money on the children – it was a way of expressing love toward them. Otherwise, she regards herself as being thrifty. He did notice that she was indeed careful with money on several occasions outside the church. She also asked for his support in that area, and he very much cherished her willingness to change.

As for the time spent in church, she told him that as long as both of them agree on any issue, she will respect it, and he will also have to do the same. He accepted what she told him for now, and waited to encounter similar situations to be totally convinced.

From Deborah's point of view, she noticed a few things in Alfred that puzzled her. Whenever they went out, she was the one talking and opening up. It took Alfred time to start responding back to her passionate way of conversing. However, once he started talking, he was a very good communicator. She debated whether this issue would be a problem in the future. After a couple of weeks, she found herself getting used to his way of conversing.

Another thing that Deborah noted in Alfred was his close attachment to his parents. She liked the fact that he was taking care of his aged parents, but she thought: "Will his parents be running our lives? Will they be intruding in our lives? Will he be spending a lot of time with them and ignoring his wife?" After meeting his parents on several occasions, she realized that they did indeed depend on him for many things in their daily lives. They were old and needed help. She knew that one day she may be in the same situation like his parents, and may very well need the help of her own children.

She did not see his closeness to his parents so alarming, but more as a Christian value. He respected and honored them (Exodus 20:12).

Outcome

After several months of praying, going out and interacting on various levels; they decided to get engaged. On Deborah's birthday, Alfred gave her the ring. It was a very special day for both of them.

This scenario is not typical for every relationship, but we certainly can learn from it. You may be in a totally different situation. We learn that we need to take our time in thinking and deciding on a lifelong commitment. We also learn that we are not to assume anything about our future spouse. Examine the behavior of your partner in several occasions. Make sure that his qualities are stable and not changeable depending on the circumstances. Remember that the decision that you will be making is a lifelong decision – for better or worse.

In summary, the main features that are stressed in Deborah and Alfred's story are: a) prayers; b) consultations; c) family involvement; d) maturity; and e) honesty.

John and Ann

John, 32, a chemist in a major hospital in Brooklyn, NY, was "in love" with Ann, 26. She was a recent graduate who joined his same work place two months earlier. He described how he felt when he first saw her. He passionately said, "From the first time I saw her, I was amazed. I felt that she was the one I have been looking for all my life. Her beauty was exquisite, her outgoing personality was superb, and her behavior was flawless. Why didn't I meet Ann several years back? I never thought that love-at-first-sight even existed, but it does. I never knew that it could happen to me!"

John was the kind of a person who would take his time in any major decision in his life. He was trying not to superficially build up his thoughts and decisions regarding Ann, based on her external beauty. However, he saw her every day at work, and it was very hard to just ignore her presence, or even not to think about her.

Over the next couple of months, they interacted at work and occasionally had lunch together. John's attraction to her grew, and he let his emotions lead his decisions. He decided to express his interest to her. When he did, she agreed to go out with him, so that they could get to know each other better.

In his description of Ann, John never mentioned anything about her way of interacting with him, whether she had expressed interest in him, or whether she was Christian. The truth turned out to be that Ann was using her beauty to charm John. He was one of the supervisors at work, and Ann wanted to use him to speedily climb the corporate ladder.

Ann had not expressed interest in him, but he made his own assumptions and conclusions. He found out, from a trusted friend, that she was not Christian, and that she was also going out with another supervisor! He could not believe that he was simply being used as a tool for her to attain her ambitions. He was stunned. He felt like he had been slapped on the face. For several months thereafter, he tried to get his act together, but could not. Finally, he started looking for another job, where he could regain his sanity. He settled for a less paying job, but at least he was regaining his peace bit by bit.

He was caught in the net of infatuation, which he could not foresee, because his mind was totally absorbed by "Miss Universe." Love is not blind, but if we let our senses take the lead in our decisions, then we may be prone to poor judgments and deleterious outcomes.

This story illustrates the fact that we should not be taken by the lure of external beauty, without taking into consideration the other aspects of the relationship.

St. Peter, in his first epistle (3:3-5), describes how much more important are the inner attributes, compared to outside appearances: "Do not let your adornment be *merely* outward – arranging the hair, wearing gold, or putting on *fine* apparel – rather *let it be* the hidden person of the heart, with the incorruptible *beauty* of a gentle and quiet spirit, which is very precious in the sight of God. For in this manner, in former times, the holy women who trusted in God also adorned themselves, being submissive to their own husbands." Moreover, in Hebrews 5:13-14, we read, "For everyone who partakes *only* of milk *is* unskilled in the word of righteousness, for he is a babe. But solid food belongs to those who are of full age, *that is*, those who by reason of use have their senses exercised to discern both good and evil."

These last two verses describe the importance of being skilled spiritually in order to differentiate right from wrong, and the good from the bad. The more we are trained spiritually, the more our decision-making process will be refined, and tuned to the will of God and His commandments.

Andrew and Sarah

Sarah, 22, and living in Chicago, was in the process of getting engaged to Andrew, 27. They planned to get married in a year. They were physically attracted to each other. He was handsome and athletic; and she was lively, outgoing, and liked by everyone. It was a done deal. For them not to get married was unimaginable. However, their relationship somehow took an unhealthy turn; and they eventually isolated themselves, and were consumed with desire for each other. What had been for them a beautiful bond became primarily a physical lust. They were so immersed in their romantic and physical relationship that they were blinded to the reality of the other person. Her close friends tried to warn her that the two of them had totally different personalities; yet she was giving them a deaf ear. Because of her inattentiveness, it took Sarah an entire year to wake up, and get to know Andrew for who he truly was. She eventually discovered things in his personality that she could not tolerate.

She abruptly broke up with him, after two years of being together. He was so devastated that it took him many months to pick up the pieces and move on with his life. Whenever his friends saw him, they saw the sorrow and hurt in his eyes from what he went through. As for Sarah, she was overwhelmed. She transferred to a different college and found support in the church, as well as from new friends.

Sarah and Andrew's story illustrates how romantic and physical involvement can cause a couple to be blinded from seeing the other for who he or she truly is. The original aim of their relationship (to marry) was appropriate, but the road toward that goal strayed off course.

I-95 Love

Alex, 30, a surgical Resident in New Jersey, USA, was getting to know Julia, 27. She was from Boston, and had a degree in biomedical engineering. They met at a get-together at his friend's house the previous summer.

When they met, they chatted for quite some time. They realized that they had many things in common. He was an adventurous person who liked to skydive and mountain climb. Julia was a deep-sea diver, and her father was a captain in the marines. They exchanged contact information in the hopes of keeping in touch. Over the next few months, they kept in touch via emails and sporadic phone calls. They had a chance to meet again at a wedding at her church in Boston. At the reception, they had the opportunity to talk, and his impression of her did not change.

He was leaning toward getting to know her more; but he was very hesitant. His residency would finish in a couple of years and she, being in Boston – 4-hour car ride away – made the situation tougher. He spoke with his spiritual guide about the situation. They prayed and waited to see how things will progress. He also spoke with his father about it (his mother passed away five years earlier). He was supportive and used to joke about his travels to Boston on Interstate-95, as "Interstate-95 love."

Alex decided to try to see her more and observe her interactions in different situations in order to decide if he should pursue a relationship with her. Whenever he had a weekend off, he would drive up north on I-95 and see her in her church.

Alex's doubts

The more he saw her in Church, the more he became comfortable with her behavior. He was happy with the positive attributes that several people mentioned about her. She was intelligent, had a strong personality, and was very determined when it came to her life goals.

However, he started to have some doubts. "Will she be stubborn, difficult to deal with, and adamant in her opinions? Will things work out with her strong-willed personality? Will I live in harmony with her? Who will take care of the house, the kids, and all the responsibilities that come with marriage?"

Alex was a goal-oriented person too. He was planning to finish his residency, start working in an office, pay off his loans, and open up his own practice. As a surgeon, it meant a lot of hours away from home. He will be surely helping her. On the other hand, at certain times, his work could be a priority – especially when he is on call, or if there are hospital emergencies. He liked her, but those doubts bothered him.

After four months of the Interstate-95 routine, and

considering all his doubts about her, he thought: "I have to talk to her to see if she shares my feelings, and if this relationship has any potential."

Vicky in the picture

When Alex's father asked him more about Julia, he realized that his answers always referred to her hobbies, and not her character. His father expressed his concern – that it seemed that Alex was more attracted to Julia's hobbies than to Julia's personality and character. He waited a couple of weeks to see how Alex handles this new insight.

When his father saw Alex in a healthy mindset to pursue a serious relationship, he directed his attention to Vicky, 30. She attended their church in New Jersey, and she was totally different from Julia. She was kind, quiet, simple and non-adventurous. She liked to read, spend time at home, and only traveled occasionally. Alex was totally against the idea of pursuing Vicky, as his father suggested, since she was not as adventurous and outgoing as Julia.

A few weeks later, during Lent, Alex saw Vicky in church. She was helping an elderly couple out of her car in the parking lot. He found himself also helping them out of the car as well. He used to just say hello and go his way, but this time, something made him talk with her.

What he saw made him realize that he really hadn't known Vicky for who she truly was. He said to himself, "What I saw today I have not seen in Julia. This quality of Vicky's is valuable and hard to find." He spoke with his dad, who looked at him with a smirk on his face and said, "Was it your guardian angel that opened your eyes today?" Alex decided to pray more fervently concerning his decision between pursuing Vicky, or Julia.

A few weeks later, he saw Vicky early in church, interacting pleasantly with people, young and old. He went home and said to his dad, "I-95 is too risky, I should stick to local highways." He spoke with his spiritual father about her, and he highly recommended Vicky for him.

Subsequently, he made a conscious effort to try to get to know her more, and to see her in different situations. He found in her a true compassionate, caring and trustworthy woman. It became clearer to him that he would be far happier with Vicky. After several months of prayers, guidance, and interactions, he expressed his interest to her.

Alex's scenario shows that continuous interactions in different situations are crucial to really get to know someone. As time goes on, we can certainly make a better and wiser decision. Furthermore, to be impressed by someone's hobby, work, or status, is one thing; but knowing the character and essence of the person is far more important for the purpose of marriage.

We also learn that we need to have someone who can give us feedback and keep us in-check. Oftentimes, the best person to help us may be a family member, or a very close and trusted friend. Lastly, life-altering decisions need to be made only when the mind and soul are calm, and in touch with our Heavenly Father.

"Husbands, love your wives, just as Christ also loved the church and gave Himself for her" (Ephesians 5:25).

14

A Time for Every Purpose

Lydia, 28, living in Orlando, FL, was sitting in her living room, when her mother walked in with a smile. Her mother asked, "Do you know that your cousin Mary is getting married in six months?" "I know mom. Please don't start," Lydia replied. "I know I am twenty-eight and that many of my friends and relatives are already married, but everything has its time under the sun. Besides, I am very busy with work and my life in general – so please don't push it."

"Mom, I know that God has a plan for me just like He had for you. I just have to wait and use my time effectively, until He reveals another plan for my life. I'm not too old to get married, and I didn't miss the boat. Don't think I'm going to go church hopping, bar hopping, or consult one of those matchmaking services to find the "right" person. I don't need someone to fill any gaps in my life, and I'm not going to fill gaps in anyone's life either. Only God, and no one else, can satisfy our needs. He created us with a mutual interest for each other. He intended for us not to live as islands – totally separated from each other, but to unite with one another and raise families glorifying His name."

Lydia's mother interrupted her and said, "Life is not

just work, school, church, and going to the gym. I thank God for your father because he was the right person for me, and we needed each other. We helped each other grow, and I don't want you to miss out on the opportunity of meeting a good man like when I met your father. The love and joy, which marriage can bring to a couple, are far beyond what the media, the senses, or the material life could bring. Marriage can contribute to your growth, your personality and the lives of others."

The Circle

Lydia did not want to be controlled by her emotions. She wanted the Holy Spirit to guide her. She hoped to find this guidance through the voice of some of her good friends, or leaders in the church. She started talking with a few of them to support her during this decision-making phase. She, and some of her close girlfriends, initiated what they called "the Circle." Three of them were engaged, while the other three were single.

The Circle benefited these friends in several ways. They met every two to three weeks to read the Bible and discuss various social issues that affected their lives. They helped each other grow spiritually, and live holy and sanctified lives for the Lord. They also discouraged those who were engaged from getting swept up in the emotions of being "in love." They recognized that, being wrapped up in that feeling, might blind a person from seeing the reality of their situation. As for those you were single, they learned valuable lessons from the negative and positive experiences of their engaged friends.

A special fact that alarmed of them was the nearly 50% divorce rate in the USA.[1] The group also learned that almost 1.2 million people were divorced in America in 1997.[2] They wondered how many of them got divorced because of impulsive decisions to get married. Such a sobering statistic offered these women another incentive to approach marriage all the more cautiously.

Friends' advice

Those who were engaged were still in the process of getting to know their future spouses. They offered some advice from which the rest of the group can benefit.

1. *Pray continuously.* Your spiritual growth is of prime importance. Be guided by your spiritual father, and do not neglect the Sacraments.

2. *It is not advisable to rush into marriage.* Discovering a person's true character often takes time. One should not bet the rest of her life on a short engagement or "pre-engagement" period.

3. *It is very important to maintain your own individual interests, and to share them.* Try not to let your own life, and identity, be consumed by your fiancé's life. The reverse is also true.

4. *It is not right to let romance be the most important aspect of your relationship.* It can distract you from real concerns and practical issues. Remember, romance can blind you from reality. Moreover, the intensity of romance during the engagement period may gradually fade or change after marriage.

5. *Guard your heart.* Keep a very cautious eye on it. Many times the heart will not listen to what the mind is advising. The individual may then live according

to the heart's desires, irrespective if they were right or wrong.

6. *During the engagement, it is vital to involve a neutral person (or couple) to whom you will be accountable for your conduct.* The person, whom you involve, if chosen wisely, will help you avoid mistakes and pitfalls in your relationship. It is also critical to maintain communications with a spiritual guide.

7. *Being involved in a relationship does not mean that you can have your guard down for whatever reason.* Examine well the progress of the relationship (whether negative or positive), and evaluate your own conduct. Be honest with yourself. Take your time, set limits, and always have the relationship in light of God's commandments.

8. *It is crucial to set physical boundaries – no sex or intimate physical relations.* Nothing on earth is worth the value of your chastity and purity. It is also wise to set emotional boundaries – not to be totally preoccupied and emotionally wrapped-up by your fiancé. Another very important point is not to feed a crush that may fire up the relation.

9. *It is absolutely unacceptable to cohabitate.*

10. *It is important to observe* how your fiancé treats his family, friends, and colleagues in different situations.

11. *Do not assume anything* about your fiancé, without confirming it in his behavior, on several occasions.

For example, one of the women saw wine bottles in her fiancé's car. She disregarded the situation initially, but then she saw more bottles every weekend. She started questioning herself: "Is he an alcoholic?" She then asked him. It turned out that his brother, who borrowed his car often, had a drinking problem.

Another woman noticed that her fiancé acted strangely whenever they went out to eat at a particular restaurant. She did not pay it too much attention, but when it recurred, she had to ask him about his behavior. He informed her that the restaurant owner was the father of his ex-fiancée, and he did not feel comfortable eating there. She apologized, and offered that he should have explained his reluctance. She was now more appreciative that he took her to her favored restaurant, despite his antipathy.

12. *Both families need to be aware of the progress of the relationship.* You need the blessings and guidance of your parents.

13. *Pre-marital counseling could be very beneficial.* It may help address certain areas of your relationship. It may also explore the strengths and weaknesses of the individuals.

Lydia's time to change

Lydia believed – being twenty-eight years old and single – was a good time to evaluate her life, goals, and above all, her spiritual growth. She also needed to evaluate what she can offer her future life partner. She wanted to refine her qualities, and acquire some values that would remain with her. However, she knew it would be very difficult to change after marriage, and if there were any self-improvements to be made, she had better work on them now before starting a family. For example, Lydia believed that, in marriage, she would not only be responsible for her own spiritual well being, but also would be supporting the spiritual growth of her family. She needed to have a stronger spiritual foundation. Furthermore, managing her daily activities with her new family, with all its responsibilities, would be another facet that needed work. She pondered all these issues and the many other challenges she would face.

She considered this period of her life as an opportunity, and a training ground for her future family life. For example, she wanted to work with disabled children. She always thought of them and their lives. This type of work sparked certain maternal feelings, and opened her eyes to problems that she had never been exposed to before.

Lydia's thoughts often turned to Rebekah, in the Old Testament. Rebekah did not spend her time trying to find a husband, rather she occupied herself serving others and developing herself into what God wanted her to become. She was waiting on the Lord and His perfect timing.

In another conversation with her parents, Lydia said, "If a baby is born premature, he will not be ready for life outside his mother's womb. He may not survive, even with medical intervention. There are issues in life that need hastiness, while there are other issues that need patience."

> "To everything *there is* a season,
> A time for every purpose under heaven:
> A time to be born, And a time to die;
> A time to plant, and a time to pluck *what is* planted."
> "He has made everything beautiful in its time…"
> (Ecclesiastes 3:1-2, 11).

Options

While you are single, and not planning to be involved with someone at this stage of your life, use the time to glorify the Lord. You do not need to get entangled in dating someone, or being obsessed over marriage. Do something productive within your community, church, or among friends. Reach out to others and help. Try to be involved in a productive service that will build your inner self. Renew old friendships. Travel, gain new friends, and understand different cultures. Read the Bible in depth with study guides. Read spiritual books, and other materials that will edify you. Start learning a new language. Excel at any type of sport, and go for the gold medal. Learn how to play a musical instrument. Collect artwork. If you are still in school, inquire about an exchange student program. Volunteer in one of the Christian missions abroad. Volunteer in a hospital, orphanage, or nursing home. Learn different kinds of crafts, and teach the younger generation. Be a photographer and enjoy the different scenes of nature and architecture. If you enjoy writing, you may compose poems or short stories.

Finally, instead of asking in any situation, "What will I get out of it?" Ask yourself and others, "How can I help?" Give, and keep giving. " ... 'It is more blessed to give than to receive' " (Acts 20:35).

Where is My Happiness?

Many people whom we have encountered in life are so eager to get married. They are totally absorbed by the idea of marriage, and the only thing that they ever talk about is who would be the perfect match for them. They do not take into consideration the responsibilities and commitment that is inherent to marriage. Parents, relatives and friends pressure some to get married quickly – or else they would "miss out."

Many of those who took a hasty and irrational decision to get married, regretted it later, and wished they had been single once again. They were not happy either way.

There is also a misconception that our appearance, possessions, or someone else can make us happy and complete. However, the reality is that none of these can make us truly joyful, or give us a sense of self-worth. We need to understand, and always be conscious of the fact, that we are complete and whole in the Lord Jesus Christ.

Notes

1. National Center for Health Statistics (NCHS) 2005 statistics.

2. U.S. Census Bureau, National Center for Health Statistics, Americans for Divorce Reform, Centers for Disease Control and Prevention, Institute for Equality in Marriage, American Association for Single People, Ameristat, Public Agenda).

15

Advice in Deciding Whom to Marry

"And God blessed them, saying, "Be fruitful and
multiply, and fill the waters in the seas, and let
birds multiply on the earth" (Genesis 1:22).

Deciding on whom to marry, and when to marry, are two crucial decisions that may very well determine how the rest of your life will turn out. If your decision is a godly one, your life will be filled with love, peace, and joy. However, if your decision is based on immaturity, impatience and mere feelings, your life may not turn out as you originally had hoped.

The following are real life examples of couples' choices and outcomes, demonstrating how crucial this decision can be:

Marilyn, 33, described her husband, Paul, 38, as the most pleasant and authentic person she had ever known. She referred to him as the man of her dreams – the only man for her. Marilyn's sister told her that she had never seen her so happy in all her life. Her husband offered unconditional love, and she felt secured by his warmth and presence. She believed that their solid relationship could, with the grace of God, withstand any obstacle that life would bring.

On the other hand, Clark, 37, described his marriage as a "disaster." He met his wife, Cynthia, 34, at a wedding. She seemed polite, friendly, and down to earth. She appeared to be the kind of person he was looking for, and everything he hoped to find. Soon after they met, they made the impulsive decision to get married. Later, Cynthia proved to be someone completely different from Clark's image of her. She wanted to control every aspect of their marriage, and was unbearably demanding. She constantly placed her needs and personal interests above his. His love and respect for her began to diminish. He even discovered that she was having an extra-marital affair, and her late nights at work were really a cover-up for her infidelity. Their lives became a battleground, and finally they were divorced.

In contrast to the previous example, a spouse with Biblical values, and a godly conscience will be a cornerstone for the success of a marriage. St. John Chrysostom (4th century A.D.) described that Rebekah was loved by Isaac for the good qualities which she brought with her from home. It was her virtues, beauty, generosity and kindness that made her such a wonderful woman.

Philippians 1:9-11 says, "And this I pray, that your love may abound still more and more in knowledge and all discernment, that you may approve the things that are excellent, that you may be sincere and without offense till the day of Christ, being filled with fruits of righteousness which *are* by Jesus Christ, to the glory and praise of God." If you grow in the love of God, your knowledge and understanding of Him will increase. If you focus on the Lord, the Creator, He will guide you, and reveal to you, which one of His children is to be your future spouse.

The following are some additional suggestions to guide you in selecting a spouse:

1. <u>Choose a man/woman of God.</u>

You need to ask yourself: "Is the Lord his or her main concern?" Are being a true Christian and being faithful to the Lord essential goals of his life? If your spouse is not a spiritual person, it will be difficult for you to persuade him to attend liturgy, church services, meetings, prayers, and the like. It will be a constant battle that may eventually lead to resentment and arguments. Does she serve the Lord – not only in church – but also in her daily living? Is God an essential part of your future spouse's life? Does she try to read the Bible regularly, and live a life of prayer? If spiritual growth is not a primary goal of your future spouse's life, will you still be willing to marry her?

Someone may then say: "What about the millions of marriages that do not have half of the previously mentioned characteristics, and they are still happy?" We do not know everyone's secrets. People are at varying stages in their relationships with God. We should not be comparing ourselves with others, who may not be as spiritual; but rather live our lives based on the commandments of God. Our temporary life on earth is the beginning of our life in heaven, and we live for Him who died for us. Consider also this life on earth as a bridge to pass to heaven. Put this idea to test, and watch the behavior of people who live on earth with heavenly conduct, versus others who live with non-heavenly conduct. Decide for yourself with whom you would rather be.

2. <u>Observe his/her behavior.</u>

Stephanie, 24, was very eager for her spiritual leader to

meet her fiancé. She always talked about what a wonderful man he was. She was advised to observe how he treats other people. Although no one is perfect, there are certain weaknesses one is willing to accept in her spouse. Conversely, there are certain traits in your future spouse with which you would not be able to live. Some questions need to be considered: "Does he lose his temper when he gets angry or upset? How does he treat you in public? How does he treat his parents? Does he go out of his way to help others? Do others respect him? Is he humble, modest and sincere? Is he stubborn or judgmental? Does he look for people's faults?"

Learn – as much as you can – by observing your future spouse in different situations, and decide if his characteristics are acceptable to you. Note that at times, the reasons for a certain action are not always apparent, or may change according to the circumstances.

3. Know that what you see is what you get.

Do not deceive yourself into thinking that you have the ability to change your future life partner. Your future spouse may be able to change some facets of his or her personality, but it's very likely that any changes will be minimal, or short-lived. Habits are difficult to change. A permanent and true behavior modification is only possible if it is based on personal conviction, and an internal desire to change. Be careful not to convince yourself that your partner's love for you is enough to inspire him or her to change his lifestyle, or personality.

Do not give excuses, deny, or sugarcoat the other person's character flaws, or weaknesses. Avoiding or covering up such faults will not prevent them from resurfacing in the future. They could become major impediments to a successful relationship.

Finally, do not relate to him based on an image of what you hope he may become. There is no Mr. Perfect or Miss Perfect. Do not deal with him according to your hopes or daydreams, but to what he truly represents.

4. <u>Ensure that you communicate well.</u>

Sound communication is one of the most important keys to a successful marriage. The media defines the quality of a relationship, and the way couples communicate, primarily in light of romantic and sexual terms. These emotions sweep the couple along, sometimes toward marriage – without getting a chance to really test their communication skills. They may also lock themselves in their relationship, without gaining from the experience of interacting with different people. However, once the couple gets married, and the romance is not as it used to be; the husband and wife may then realize that they have difficulty communicating.

> Sandy, 23 and engaged, wanted to talk to her spiritual guide about her communication problems with her fiancé. Her spiritual guide asked her, "Don't you discuss everything openly with him?" She replied, "No, we don't really talk about much."

Sandy went out with him her fiancé, to fulfill her needs of belonging, intimacy and love. She ignored the fact that it is very important for her to grow intellectually, as well as spiritually, with him.

You could be romantically attracted to your partner, and you could like many of his qualities; however, do you communicate well with each other? Do you have difficulty getting your message across? Do you understand each other easily? Moreover, when you have disagreements, do you try to understand the other person's point of view, or does each person insist on having their way? A difference in educational background may also prove to be an obstacle – leading to clashes and misunderstandings.

If any disagreements happen before marriage, it may actually be a beneficial, eye-opening experience that will reveal a couple's differences. Recognizing differences before marriage, in turn, prepares each person to address, resolve and manage those issues.

> Marguerite always appreciated her neighbors, Mr. and Mrs. Jacobson, an elderly couple who recently celebrated their sixtieth wedding anniversary. They were almost inseparable. They had their share of disagreements, but they always talked out their problems, and eventually come to a resolution to their disputes. They always communicated with respect and love. They were inseparable, and behaved as one.

5. <u>How about your spouse's emotional and psychological maturity?</u>

Maturity is critical to a sound marriage. Does your future spouse possess an independent character, or does he or she tend to follow the crowd out of insecurity? Does she know how to control negative emotions, or does she lose control? Is he primarily preoccupied with feelings and romance, and tends to shun away from mature conversations?

Living with such a person will lead to a very unbalanced, unfulfilled and frustrating life. You may find yourself "baby-sitting" your spouse – prompting them as to what they should say or do – and unable to interact with him at a mature level.

6. What are your spouse's views on family?

You need to know if your future spouse is truly looking forward to parenthood. This issue needs to be discussed openly so that a clear understanding is reached.

Besides deciding on whether or not to have children, you need to know whether the future father or mother of your children has good family values. Is he prepared and willing to raise children to be the Lord's? Remember, family will be one of the most important aspects of your future; you will need help raising God-fearing children.

Is he going to be dedicated to his family? Is he the kind of person who would be willing to sacrifice his own life for his family's well being?

> "Husbands, love your wives, just as Christ also loved the church and gave Himself for her" (Ephesians 5:25).

7. Seek guidance and advice from loved ones.

If you have reached the appropriate stage to be in a relationship with someone, try to seek the advice of your priest, spiritual counselor, parents, or close friends. Your guidance may come from one or a few individuals who are equipped to give sound advice and help you make the best decisions. It is wiser to be guided and prevent mistakes, than not to be guided and regret making a series of blunders.

Lastly, do not expect that the advice that you will be offered will always be what you want to hear – it may be the complete opposite. Nevertheless, be receptive; and remember that the one offering you the advice is someone who cares about you and wants the best for you. Through prayers and guidance, you can easily come up with a solution that will be best for the situation you are facing.

8. Confirm his beliefs, attitudes and values.

Understanding the other person's beliefs and values is an important element in getting to know your future spouse. Are his values based on a solid foundation, or do they waver depending on the circumstance? How long has your future spouse held her particular views? Were they recently acquired to impress you? Does your future spouse keep his word? Are her values consistent with the teachings of the Scriptures and the Church?

Bridgett, 31, was in the process of getting engaged to Patrick, 35. She met him four months earlier at a spiritual convention. Initially he seemed to be a man who loves the Lord from all his heart, and lead a holy life. He met her family, and they started going out together. Some warning signs began to surface; but she ignored them.

One time, Patrick invited her to go on a fishing trip with him and a few friends. Bridgett viewed this trip as a golden opportunity to observe Patrick and his relationship with others. She was wise in asking her brother, Michael, 24, to come with her. She wanted someone, whom she trusted, to help her identify if there are truly some warning signs, or they were from her imagination. She wanted her brother to provide an honest advice. The first day of the trip went well. However, the next day, Patrick left her alone and went to a nearby town without mentioning a word to her. When he finally returned, Bridgett asked him about his sudden disappearance. Patrick instantly snapped at her and said, "You are not my wife! That's none of your business!" She was shocked at his response. Her brother was surprised, when he knew about Patrick's behavior. That same night, Bridgett and Michael prayed together and asked God to reveal His will, sooner than later. The following day, Patrick pulled the same disappearing act again, but this time when he returned, he smelled of alcohol. That was a message from

God through Bridgett's guardian angel. She realized that Patrick did not live according to the values and morals she believed he had. She thanked God for revealing to her the true nature of this man. Upon receiving this epiphany from God, Bridgett and Michael packed their belongings and left the next morning.

Patrick's values, that initially seemed holy, were not what she thought. Patrick's aggressiveness and drinking were masked by a behavior that seemed loving and spiritual. The pressure and challenge of the situation he faced, unmasked his true essence.

9. <u>Do not expect or assume things about your partner.</u>

Colleen, 34, had been seeing Randolph, 39, for a few months. He was working as a corporate executive at a large firm in San Francisco, CA. Colleen was very happy with him, his personality, and the way he treated her. As their courtship progressed, she became more and more convinced that he was the right man for her.

One evening, while dining at a lavish restaurant, a lady approached their table and introduced herself as Randolph's wife! Colleen was dumbfounded. He never had a ring on his finger, and never had spoken about his past. After her initial shock set in, she grabbed her things and stormed out of the restaurant with tears and a broken heart.

Colleen's experience reveals the naïveté in not seeking answers to questions we may have about our future partner. One should not be afraid to ask questions of her future spouse, and listen attentively to the answers. Examine the truthfulness of your partner's responses by paying attention to whether those responses remain constant, or whether they change depending on the circumstances, occasions or mood. In addition, Colleen did not try to involve her parents, nor her spiritual father. She was not getting any support, during her relationship, to help her think properly and wisely.

10. <u>Know well what personality/lifestyle suits you.</u>

    Karen, 26, was totally different from Mark, 30. She was the extroverted and independent type with many hats in her bag. He was the shy and quiet type who did not like to take risks.

    What type of personality are you most comfortable with? Is it the quiet, shy type, who likes to stay home and enjoy a modest social life? Are you more compatible with the outgoing, energetic, adventurous type; or do you prefer the tough, strong, and direct person? What about the emotional and sentimental personality? Will you leave decision-making to your partner, or do you need to control and influence every matter? Do you enjoy sports and other physical activities, or is relaxing at home in front of the fireplace more appealing? You need to discover which of these best fits your personality.

11. <u>Look for the inner qualities.</u>

    The way your future spouse looks and dresses, most certainly should not be the primary factor in your decision-making process. If you base your decision on images you see on television, movies, or magazines, you will be disappointed. Try to separate what you observe in the media from your expectations for marriage. If you compare your future spouse's physical attributes, with the appearance of movie stars and celebrities, and how they present themselves in public, then you may ultimately be disappointed.

Psalm 45:13 states, "The royal daughter *is* all glorious within *the palace*; Her clothing *is* woven with gold." The Psalmist was describing that the glory of the human soul is within the palace, which is your heart or your deepest inner thoughts. This inner beauty is the reflection of the light of the Lord Jesus Christ on the human soul. It is deeper, and more valuable, than the fading illusion of all the fake earthly glories, pleasures and outward appearances.

16

Pitfalls in Choosing Whom to Marry

"For your Maker *is* your husband, The LORD of hosts *is* His name; And your Redeemer *is* the Holy One of Israel; He is called the God of the whole earth" (Isaiah 54:5).

There is no doubt that every one of us desires to live a happy and healthy life. Unfortunately, our society and the media teach us to rely on our instincts and feelings. However, emotions and romantic feelings alone do not offer a strong foundation for a long lasting relationship. Rather, they may distract a person from examining the issues and concerns that are indispensable to a successful marriage.

When contemplating this critical decision to pursue a relationship, one needs to be vigilant, use sound discretion, and seek the Lord's will, through prayer and guidance. In the process of making this life-changing decision, we can learn from mistakes that others have made. The following are some of these pitfalls.

1. <u>Now, not later</u>

A "now" decision is when you hastily decide to enter into a serious commitment, after a short time of getting to know the other person. To get married after only a few months of getting to know each other is generally not advisable.

We can compare this situation to someone opening the curtains of a window. As he slightly opens the curtain, he sees a partial and incomplete image of the world outside. As he opens that curtain further, he can see more of the view. It is risky to make the hasty decision to get married, based on only a fraction of your future spouse's true image.

Making the decision to marry "later" (within a reasonable time) in your courtship, will offer you the opportunity to know your future spouse more completely. Take enough time to pray about this very important decision. We need faithful prayers, patience, and submission to the Almighty Conductor of our lives, whose music is well orchestrated and flawless; just try listening to it.

2. <u>Young and attractive</u>

David, 20, saw in Melissa, 17, the exquisite beauty found in a Miss Universe contestant. He chose to be with her, because all he cared about was being with someone who was physically attractive – whose outward splendor turned heads.

Don't let your youthful energy guide you to what is merely outward "attractiveness," while disregarding the more important inner attributes of the person. External beauty fades in time; but the true, genuine essence of the individual, is like gold being refined day after day. In addition, deciding to get married at such a young age of 20 and 17 is a risk – since maturity is one of the essential cornerstones for the success of marriage.

"Charm *is* deceitful and beauty *is* passing, But a woman *who* fears the LORD, she shall be praised" (Proverbs 31:30).

3. <u>Wrong reasons</u>

Cathy, 24, found in Solomon, 31, the wealthy man who could give her all the luxuries life can offer. When she saw Solomon's expensive car, his flashy wardrobe, and expensive accessories, she was mesmerized with the idea of living the comfortable life, of which she had always dreamed. She had been brought up in a very modest home, and she resented it. Once she was introduced to Solomon, she never let him out of her sight. She constantly called him, and tried to spend as much time with him as possible.

For her, money and wealth were the most important considerations for starting a family. Three months later, Cathy and Solomon set a wedding date.

In addition to wealth, we can enumerate other wrong motives for getting married; like fear, loneliness, sexual desire, getting old, and pressure from family and friends.

"They told me to"

Sometimes people's decisions are based on what others think. However, it's not always right to make personal decisions in order to please others.

Martha, 25, was from a very loving, yet authoritative family. They tried to control her decisions despite her resistance. Her father had recently passed away, and her mother became very worried about Martha's future. The last thing Martha wanted was to displease her family, especially after her father's death.

Her mother began introducing her to many men in the hopes of finding her a husband. In the beginning, Martha strongly resisted, but eventually agreed to get to know one particular gentleman, Raymond. After three months of courtship, her mother had already selected the wedding date, and planned the entire ceremony.

Martha and Raymond married. But Martha, who always had an angelic smile on her face, became miserable, and has forgotten how to be happy. Her mother did not understand, or respect, the fact that it was Martha's decision to choose the person with whom she will share the rest of her life.

4. <u>Cupid's fault</u>

Marisa, 22, fell "madly in love" with Steve, 26, since she first met him at her cousin's graduation party. They started seeing each other, and became very emotionally involved. She had never experienced that type of "love" before, and asked herself, "What else do I need? How fantastic was Cupid who drove his arrow into my heart!"

Driven by her emotions, she eventually married Steve, (but actually, she married "Cupid"). After two months of marriage, she complained, "It is all Cupid's fault. I never hated myself so much, or felt so ignorant, since I decided to marry Steve. He doesn't care about me anymore, and most of the time, he is either with his friends or at work. He only needs me and shows me affection when he wants to be intimate. Sometimes I feel like a mere ornament, and at times, even like a piece of trash. I can see that I don't have a place in his heart anymore; it's a living hell."

It is apparent that the Lord Jesus did not exist at all in their marriage, and the Church had a minimal effect on their lives. It was "Cupid" who had all the effect on her.

5. <u>Having an unbalanced life</u>

You need to live a balanced and mature life with your whole being (body, soul, and spirit). Are your spirit, soul, and body whole? Which one of these is controlling you? Is your spirit guiding you to a holy life? Is your soul leading you to an instinct-oriented life? Is your body yearning to what is sinful? You are the one who can truly know what is leading your life. It is within your power, with God's grace, to change for the better – to live a holy and blameless life before the Lord.

> "Now may the God of peace Himself
> sanctify you completely;
> and may your whole spirit, soul, and body
> be preserved blameless
> at the coming of our Lord Jesus Christ"
> (1 Thessalonians 5:23).

Samantha, 35, was married to André, 41; and they had two kids. She was promoted four months earlier to director at a reputable New York firm. She was ecstatic, and was eager to prove herself. She started staying late at work almost daily. The kids hardly see her during the week. She even started skipping church activities, or she went late when she did go.

Several times, André spoke with her about returning home late. Finally, she agreed to come home early. However, due to her ambitious aspirations, she was not able to keep her promise. Her husband could not sit and watch, while the situation was getting worse. He had another talk with her, and they discussed more openly the same concerns. She again promised to leave work on time to be with her family. However, deep inside, she was not sure if she would be able to, since she had so many commitments at work. She was eager to climb the executive ladder. She was consumed by her ambitions while her responsibilities at home, and at church, became less important. Her marriage, as well as her spirituality, was suffering.

Our lives need to be balanced. It is not healthy (on any level) to pay more attention to any one particular aspect of our lives – whether it is your soul, body, or spirit – and neglect the other two aspects. A well-balanced and well-rounded life is crucial for the success of any relationship, and will guarantee a healthier marriage.

Tertullian[1], an early Church Father, wrote a letter (202 A.D.) to his wife, illustrating the great esteem for the Mystery of Holy Matrimony:

> "How beautiful, then, the marriage of two Christians, two who are one in hope, one in desire, one in the way of life they follow, one in the religion they practice. They are as brother and sister, both servants of the same Master. Nothing divides them, either in flesh or in Spirit. They are in every truth, two in one flesh; and where there is but one flesh there is also but one spirit.
>
> They pray together, they worship together; they fast together; instructing one another; encouraging one another; strengthening one another. Side by side they face difficulties and persecution, share their consolations. They have no secrets from one another, they never shun each other's company; they never bring sorrow to each other's hearts. Psalms and hymns they sing to one another.
>
> Hearing and seeing this, Christ rejoices. To such as these He gives His peace. Where there are two together, there also He is present, and where He is, there evil is not."

Notes

1. Ante-Nicene and Post-Nicene Fathers Series.

Concluding Thoughts

The goal of this book is to help relay a Biblical viewpoint on dating, relationships and engagement. Regarding these topics, we need to live our lives in light of the words of our heavenly Father, whose love for us is beyond measure. At the same time, we are to enjoy His presence in our lives.

Our search for our marriage partner will lead us to kneel down at the feet of our Savior, and humbly ask Him to show us His way. Strive to hear God's voice, and He will reveal Himself to you. God has a plan for each one of us to be fulfilled in His time.

I do pray from all my heart that each page, each sentence, each word, and each letter of this book, be used for the glory of the Lord. Finally, I do request that you pray for the writer that he may be granted to serve Him more and more, till the last breath.

May the Lord guide all of us to live with Him, by Him, and for Him.

N.B. The writer welcomes your feedback on this book.
Email address: drgbassaly@gmail.com